The World Is a Nice Place

The World Is a Nice Place

HOW TO OVERCOME ADVERSITY, JOYFULLY

—

Amy Molloy

HAY HOUSE, INC.

Carlsbad, California • New York City
London • Sydney • Johannesburg
Vancouver • New Delhi

Published and distributed in Australia by: Hay House Australia Pty. Ltd.: www.hayhouse.com.au
Published and distributed in the United States by: Hay House, Inc.: www.hayhouse.com

Published and distributed in the United Kingdom by: Hay House UK, Ltd.: www.hayhouse.co.uk
Published in India by: Hay House Publishers India: www.hayhouse.co.in

Design by Rhett Nacson
Typeset by Bookhouse, Sydney
Edited by Margie Tubbs
Author Photo by Jody Pachniuk

ISBN: 978-1-4019-5087-3
Digital ISBN: 978-1-4019-5088-0

10 9 8 7 6 5 4 3 2 1
1st edition, April 2018

To my Special Chosen One,
and my Special Gifted One.

Thank you for waiting for me.

Contents

PROLOGUE

Too Much, Too Young?

Challenging, difficult, unpredictable, a magnet for drama. These are some of the terms my family would use to (flatteringly) describe my younger years. The first quarter of my life can be best described as . . . eventful. It's only when I list my trials in chronological order that I grasp their gravitas completely. From a dangerously premature baby, I became a child with obsessive-compulsive tendencies, a teenager with an eating disorder and a 23-year-old widow. Throw in a family history of depression, a father paralysed from cancer, and a tendency to have spiritual premonitions and that's a recipe for a messed-up adult. Or is it?

I'm writing this as a 33-year-old happy, healthy woman with a baby growing in my belly, a fulfilling career and a loving relationship with my parents and partner. I'm not perfect—and proud of it—but I am certainly not broken, regretful or downtrodden. Against the odds, I have learnt to overcome my early hurdles without letting them become my identity, instead using them to empower and guide me. How is it possible? Well, that's what this book is all about.

As a journalist who specialises in telling real-life stories, I've spent the last fifteen years of my career tracking down amazing people who've faced amazing challenges. I've interviewed 9/11 rescue workers whose lungs have been destroyed by the dust from the Twin Towers, survivors of plane crashes and tsunami victims who've scrambled out of natural disasters. But I've also seen evidence of how 'everyday' events—particularly in our younger years—can be just as destructive to our psyche as headline-making catastrophes.

Think back to a bad patch in your past. A time when you felt deserted, desolate, tested. Have you really grown out of it? Or has it had a lasting effect on you? When you think of that memory, do your teeth clench or shoulders tense? Well, these are only the obvious side effects that you're aware of. There are so many of us out there—problem children who became troubled teenagers then grew into twenty-year-olds who just seem to attract chaos.

According to an American study of over 13,000 adults, more than 50 percent admitted that, during their childhood, they had been exposed to an 'adverse experience.'[1] This ranged from emotional distress to mental illness or separation from a parent. In these adults, researchers found an increased risk of depression, alcoholism, drug abuse and attempted suicide.

In my friendship circle, I can name (although I won't) a dozen men and women in their twenties, thirties and beyond who are still affected by difficult experiences in their younger years. They struggle to commit to relationships because of abandonment issues; they doubt their abilities because their first boss criticised them; or they hate their bodies because their first boyfriend pointed out their cellulite. I've interviewed women with infertility issues, who say they can pinpoint the trauma that 'shut down' their femininity and caused them to disconnect from their bodies. (I am one of them!)

When a person has experienced struggles in their younger years, whether it's in their childhood, teens or twenties, it can be easy to write them off as a lost cause. (What chance does she have? or It's no wonder he messed up after everything he's been through!) You may have heard this said about you. You might have said it about yourself.

Many of us have moments from our past that we're still hung up on. The person who broke your heart; the illness that thwarted your plans; the trauma that tore you apart; the opportunity that was taken from you—or that you didn't take. It's very easy to let that moment embody you, with constant revisiting, regretting or wondering what might have been. But it doesn't have to be that way.

I truly believe that an eventful upbringing doesn't have to be devastating, if we can flip our mindset and see an adverse experience as a teaching tool—even as a super-power. I'm not saying it's easy, but it is possible. I am lucky to count among my closest friends a bunch of amazing and inspiring women whose early years would make you wince. Their early experiences range from the loss of a parent, to sickness, sexual abuse and crippling shyness. Yet they have flourished into empowered, empathetic adults who haven't learnt to 'own' their past—instead they have overcome it.

In the past, I've ticked off and circled around most of the self-destructive traits one person can manifest—obsession, addiction, self-harm, isolation, burnout and excessive attachment. But I've managed to shake each monster off my back, one by one, until I am left with a version of myself that is stronger and more capable from once carrying them. Most importantly, I am vibrantly happy.

I am far from perfect, with a relationship résumé that includes three marriages (widowed at 23, divorced at 30). But I've never for a moment given up on finding a happy ending and I've always—without hesitation—been able to keep moving forwards.

Years ago, I interviewed the parents of a 26-year-old woman who now has permanent brain damage, from a failed suicide attempt when she tried to hang herself. They described their daughter as a 'troubled teen' who suffered from mood swings, never felt comfortable in her skin and struggled to recover from a relationship breakdown. That interview hit me hard, because it could have been me—it could have been so many of us. But you don't have to take your own life, to waste it by living in the past.

The title of this book is my personal motto: The world is a nice place. Whenever I feel myself beginning to drift into worry, sadness, anxiety or unease I repeat this aloud: It'll all be okay . . . because the world is a nice place. There is enough trash talk about the universe. It's trendy to say life is too hard. But I've learnt that life is much harder, if you expect it to be.

I hope this book can help you to explore your memories, pinpoint your own triggers and actually find ways to make them work in your favour. Over the next nineteen chapters, I'll share tips, coping mechanisms and positive exercises to help free you from the past and help you to thrive in the future. In my experience, early struggles can create emotionally invincible adults who have more compassion, self-confidence, self-awareness and resilience than those 'lucky' people who have never been tested.

This doesn't mean you'll come out of a struggle unscathed or unchanged. However, you will learn to appreciate the side effects that come from survival. I'm not a psychologist or an academic but I do come to this topic from a unique perspective—a lost cause who overcame adversity, recovered joyfully and turned her toughest challenges into a limitless life.

All the best people have a bad patch.

Don't give up.

Amy x

ONE

A Tough Start

As a little girl, I loved asking my mum to tell me about my birth. How the nurses wrapped my four pound body in tinfoil like a chicken and put me in an incubator to finish 'cooking' me. How I would forget to breathe in the first few weeks of life so my parents would tickle my feet to remind me to inhale. How my mum burst into tears the first time she put a nappy on me, because it came up to my chin. The night the doctors said the next eight hours were make or break. If I survived until the morning I would probably live, but the darkness might steal the last spark of my life. Their relief when, come sunrise, I was still breathing.

When I was little, I would look at photos of my younger self—pink and shrivelled in an incubator surrounded by tubes. I had defied the odds, born two and a half months early, like my older sister who joined the outside world three months before her due date. My mum has a womb abnormality called a bicornuate uterus (double vagina and double cervix). My sister and I both grew in her 'left' uterus. But with only half the room a normal baby has we both ran out of space early.

You could say it was my first act of rebellious behaviour—breaking out of the womb because my surroundings weren't serving me, with disregard for the long-term consequences. This was the first of many (many!) times that I would reduce both my parents to tears with the challenges that swirled around me.

During the first few years of my life I was hospital-ised several times, firstly for pneumonia and later when I got the blood infection septicaemia in my right arm and came close to having it amputated. I was in hospital over Christmas Day, my dad at home pulling crackers with my sister and my mum sobbing in the hospital while listening to the Salvation Army singing carols.

I gave my parents countless sleepless nights when I was a baby—but nobody blames me, nobody is angry with me and I don't feel at all guilty for what happened. Thirty years later, I am not judged because I made an unconventional entrance, or because I was a challenging baby who needed extra care and attention. It doesn't negatively affect people's view of me now or negatively affect my view of myself. I accept that it wasn't my fault that I was born early, due to a biological abnormality. It wasn't my fault that I couldn't fight a blood infection or that my parents spent much of my early years plagued with worry.

As babies, our troubles aren't held against us. They are not forgotten but they are forgiven, easily and naturally, without even having to consider them, not only by the people who love us but also by ourselves. Imagine if you could feel the same compassion and forgiveness around setbacks in your later life—if you could learn from them, grow from them and evolve from them, without ever becoming stuck or stagnant?

You could argue that we don't remember events from our babyhood, which makes it easier for us to get over them. But how much of your suffering is caused by the actual memory of an event and how much is caused by perpetual self-criticism, guilt, regret and worry about what people think of you, for being the person it has happened to?

My parents didn't give up on me because I had a difficult start to my life, nor do they blame me for causing them pain and worry. We accept that our earliest years are broken into developmental stages—some easy and some more difficult—as we grow with different stimuli and influences. It is not assumed that a difficult baby will become a difficult adult, forever defined by our weakest, most vulnerable moments.

- So, when does that change?
- At what age do we start to become stuck in our struggles?
- At what age do we stop forgiving ourselves for difficult periods?
- When do we start feeling guilty for feeling, for failing, for getting ill or not acting in a way that is perceived as normal?
- When do we begin storing up negative feelings?
- When do we start letting our past dictate our future?

Think back to your own birth and entry into this world. Were you born early, late or right on time? Did you give your mother morning sickness during her pregnancy? Did you enter the world screaming and need special care and attention? And did your parents hold these actions against you? I doubt it! They probably talk proudly about it now and even discuss the negatives as a positive (We always knew you were going to be a determined one!). Imagine if you could look back on every struggle with the same sense of acceptance, nostalgia and positivity? You can! It's within your power to do so.

You may have a dark—or at least shady—patch in your history. Perhaps you regret a decision, wish you'd taken an alternate route, or wonder how life could have been different if you hadn't met a certain person. You might carry guilt for putting your family—and yourself—through a challenging situation. You might even be angry with the person you once were (How could I have done that? How could I have been her? Why did I put all of us through that?).

Whether you faced challenges in your teens, twenties or thirties, I hope that by the end of this book you can see them as a life stage instead of a life sentence. Forgive your actions, your reactions, your responses and your learning curves. See them for what they were—transitions—and take positive lessons from them where you can.

As a premature baby, I do think my early entrance has influenced the adult that I've become. I'm perpetually early for everything and I don't have any ear lobes (apparently they're one of the last things to form in the womb). I have one weak arm from the septicaemia, which means I drift diagonally when I'm swimming. But these are just souvenirs from a life stage that is behind me.

As you begin this journey, one of the most important components is compassion. Think about yourself as a baby (stick a photo of your newborn self on your bathroom mirror if that helps you). How would you react to a baby who went through a difficult period or was born into difficult circumstances? Would you write them off as a lost cause or judge them harshly for the rest of their lives?

When I was born early, my parents were warned that premature babies can have developmental problems and often struggle to keep up intellectually with their school-friends. Instead of accepting this outcome, they had faith in my abilities. They focused on the words of one nurse in the Special Care Unit who said: 'Premature babies are born survivors. They're always tough little things.' They didn't let one stage in my life define or confine me.

All of our lives are made up of developmental stages, from the moment we are conceived to the moment we breathe our last breath. Few people are immune to growing pains along the way. As we move through this book, cradle your past, comfort yourself and know that everyone has a chance to be reborn every day.

Self-forgiveness ~
A FIVE-MINUTE MEDITATION

Sit in a comfortable position (for me that's crossed-legged on the floor with my back against a wall). Hold your hands in your lap so your fingertips are touching.

Think about all the things your fingertips have touched over a lifetime: the face of your parents when you were a baby; the first objects you held; the gravel of your school playground; the paper of a school exam; the body of your first lover; the skin of a person who you've said goodbye to.

Think about all the firsts and lasts your fingertips have touched and the highs and lows they've been part of.

Focus on the feeling of your fingertips pressing together now; one fingertip for each fingertip, no fingertip left out, perfectly matched, every fingertip supported by its opposite.

Acknowledge that you have always been a constant in your own life. You have never gone missing. You have never been far. You have always been there, right here, for every single experience.

As you feel your fingertips pressing together now, let your shoulders drop, let your jaw relax. And say 'thank you.'

TWO

Lessons from Your Lowest Point

When I was seventeen and eating just one piece of toast per week (yes, per week) supplemented by energy drinks and handfuls of sultanas, my mother gave me a piece of advice that eventually became the basis of my recovery from anorexia. 'You're so powerful,' she said. 'If only you could take the determination that you're using to starve yourself and instead channel it into something positive, then you could achieve anything. You could make magic happen.'

It was an incredible piece of advice, especially coming at my lowest weight, when it would have been easy to give up on me. I was too weak to walk up the stairs, my dad had to confiscate my car keys in case I fainted at the wheel, and I was routinely taking two packs of laxatives a day. Yet my parents saw the emotional strength behind my physical weakness. If only I could channel that power into projects that allowed me to grow rather than shrink.

I wish I could say I took my mum's advice on board. At the time, her words fell on deaf ears (and a starving stomach). Luckily, it turned out that she was right. As a happy, healthy 33-year-old I still possess many of the personality traits that made me a 'successful' anorexic: self-control, self-discipline and an overabundance of willpower. However, I have found a way to use these 'talents' to my advantage. I have turned the dogged determination that nearly killed me into the fuel that has driven my career, given me the courage to move countries and allowed me to hit almost every life goal that I've set my mind to.

I'm not the only person to have used teenage troubles to their advantage. Did you get in with the wrong crowd, dabble in drugs, withdraw into yourself, date a bad boy or act out in any way? There is evidence that adolescent angst can actually be a positive.

A study from the University of California found that troubled teenagers are more likely to become successful entrepreneurs than teenagers who have not engaged in 'risky activities' because it takes a 'unique combination of breaking rules and being smart' to handle the ups and downs of business and life in general.[1]

A separate study from Kansas State University found that people who were 'moderate rule breakers' as children—we're talking about skipping classes rather than engaging in serious crimes—were more likely to become leaders later in life.[1] There are famous examples of troubled teens who've gone onto great things—Richard Branson, Steve Jobs, and Oprah Winfrey. Elon Musk, the founder of SpaceX and Tesla, describes his entire teenage years as an 'existential crisis.'

In a TED Talk, business coach Cameron Herold argues that difficult teenagers should be encouraged into entrepreneurship, because they already possess many of the skills they need to succeed: tenacity, introspection, interdependence and a passionate set of values.

- Have you ever been criticised, or criticised yourself, for displaying the above qualities?
- Have you ever felt bad because of this side of yourself?

It's amazing how the identities we adopt as schoolchildren and teenagers can hold us back as adults. Whether you were the class clown, the class nerd, the popular or unpopular kid, the troublemaker or the teacher's pet, it can stay with you forever and constrict your opinion of yourself and the role you play in the future. I still carry guilt for the rift my disordered eating caused my family, but part of my healing has come from recognising the gifts that time in my life gave me.

How would you describe yourself as a teenager?

Think about the first sentence that comes into your head. Whose words are you using? Is that really how you think about your younger self or is it what a parent, teacher, sibling or schoolfriend once said about you?

- Who were you, really?
- What was driving that behaviour?
- What life skills were you practising in your most troubled moments?

I am not proud of the pain my eating disorder put my family through, but I am strangely proud of my teenage self, including all of her flaws and issues. From a young age, my anorexia taught me that I had a power within me to make changes, to set my mind on a mission and follow it through, regardless of the sacrifices.

I do not under any circumstances recommend starvation as a path to self development and I'm extremely lucky that my condition didn't kill me (I came closer than I ever like to admit). But I am amazed that I went to college, despite ingesting so few calories; that I never missed a day of work or asked for special privileges. I am proud that, at the worst point in my disorder, I chose to get help and then booked a one-way ticket to the other side of the world, because I sensed I needed to temporarily leave my old life behind.

My eating disorder made me an independent thinker and an answer seeker. It sparked my interest in self-development, as I searched for ways to cure myself. At the age of seventeen, I could quote Chicken Soup for the Soul, Louise Hay and Feel the Fear and Do It Anyway. I became curious, observant and self-aware, as I searched for meaning and healing.

It even put me on the path to my future career. When I was trying to recover, I carried a newspaper article in my pocket that I read before every meal to try and control my inner demons. It was an interview with a grandfather who had survived a Nazi holocaust camp. He spoke about how he was so hungry he climbed down into a pit of dead bodies to pull a half-eaten apple out of his murdered friend's pocket.

I read this article over and over again before breakfast, lunch and dinner, to force myself to feel grateful rather than anxious that I had food to eat. The author of that article will never know that he saved a teenage girl from starvation. But I remember thinking that one day I would like to write an article that would save someone else. It was my first realisation that I wanted to be a writer—the most positive decision of my life.

☐ SOMETIMES YOU HAVE TO GO OFF THE RAILS TO GET ONTO THE RIGHT TRACK

At the age of seventeen, I announced to my parents that I was dropping out of college to go travelling with the man I'd lost my virginity to (yes, that was how I explained it to them). I went as far as booking my flights and applying for a visa, before coming to my senses and ending the relationship.

That was eight weeks before my final college exams. I'd been so busy being in love that I'd only been to a handful of lectures. When I asked my teachers if I could still sit the tests they all agreed but warned me there was no way I would possibly pass them. Did I listen? Of course not! In less than two months I did a year's worth of study, handed in all of my missing assignments and passed with distinction. I had missed the cut-off date for applying to university but called the application office and begged them to consider me anyway. A few weeks I received an acceptance letter.

Perhaps it would have been simpler, and certainly less stressful, if my higher education had been more conventional. However, my detour helped me develop skills that I otherwise might not have discovered. Think back to the firsts in your life: your first important exams, your first job, your first relationship, your first act of rebellion. What did each experience teach you about yourself, your limitations and capabilities, your drivers and desires?

These days I like to think of myself as a 'responsible rebel.' I still frequently do things that make my parents gasp, 'What is she thinking?' But my risks are far more calculated and I try to rebel in the right way. I still push against authority sometimes and I still ignore the advice of people who are older and wiser than I. But it's only because I've learnt to trust my gut feelings, to listen to my inner voice and to prioritise what matters to me.

Even now, I think back to my college days whenever I'm facing a tight deadline or a task that seems impossible. I think about the teachers who said I would fail and the voice in my head which told me to try anyway. This gave me hope when, in my final year of university, I couldn't attend any lectures because I was caring for a terminal cancer patient. It gave me the stamina to write my entire thesis from the oncology ward where my husband was being treated. It gave me the courage to start a new job hosting a fashion segment on a television show just two weeks after his funeral.

It was my inner rebel who made the decision to immigrate to Australia five years ago after being offered a job in Sydney, even though I broke my mother's heart by leaving. You could say it was a selfish move and definitely a rebellious one. But I put myself first because, even when the Australian magazine I worked for closed down, my instinct told me I needed to follow my inner compass and stay here.

The reality is that not everyone will agree with all of your life choices. In hindsight, you may not agree with the life choices you've previously made. But when a decision has been and gone, the most powerful thing you can do is own it, understand it and take the positives from it.

If you've been labelled as rebellious, difficult or a trouble-maker, don't the stigma of that hold you back. There is often a misconception that any rebellion is a bad thing, but nonconforming choices can take you on an extraordinary journey. Sometimes it takes a degree of selfishness to go the distance—so forgive yourself for that.

Now that I have a baby growing in my belly, it is finally clear why I had to move across the world against some people's wishes and to fall in love with a certain man on a certain day on a continent 15,000 kilometres away from my homeland. If I hadn't rebelled, I wouldn't have conceived the child who was destined to be ours.

Your addictive personality ~
FIVE REASONS WHY IT CAN BE AN ADVANTAGE

1. You're probably very sensual.

A lot of addictive personality types have a disposition towards 'sensation seeking'—the search for experience and feelings that are varied, novel and intense. Recognise that about yourself, and then search for healthier sensations than drugs or alcohol. I go swimming in the ocean, even in the middle of winter, because the intensity of the cold water makes my head buzz and my heart race.

2. Cold turkey boosts creativity.

When I stopped starving myself, I began hungrily journalling, filling pages and pages of notebooks with diary entries, poems and doodles. Cold turkey can be the perfect time to unleash your creativity. When I began eating again, I felt like my mind had come alive and my artistic side had awoken. I also began to read ferociously, because I craved a distraction.

3. You're a strategic thinker.

When I was starving myself, I learnt to plan ahead like an army lieutenant. If I was going to an event, especially with people who I barely knew, I'd have to think ahead, survey the scene and put strategies in place to be able to hide my disordered eating habits. Today, I strategise in the same way when I go to networking events for work, but now I plan how to work the room, meet influential people who I admire, and avoid certain people who I know drag me down.

4. You're a project person.

For years, not eating was my passion project. When I gave that up, I suddenly had a lot of time and energy on my hands (anorexia is a full-time job!). I've lost count of the number of projects I've embarked on since then, from heath kicks to hobbies and volunteering work, filling the space where my demons once were. I embrace every project with the same passion and tenacity.

5. You know yourself inside out.

Because of my history with disordered eating, I'm hyper-aware of my weaknesses and I don't think that's a bad thing. I know my triggers, the type of people I need to avoid and the subtle signs that indicate I might be relapsing. I never understate the depths that I can mentally drop into, so I make sure I have a 'ladder' of coping mechanisms by my side at all times.

THREE

Happiness, Regardless

The word 'antidepressants' was part of my vocabulary before my age hit double digits. A number of adults in my family, including my mum, were long-term takers. From a young age, I knew what Prozac was and remember playing with the boxes of St John's Wort tablets that were stacked by the telephone. 'All the females in our family are crazy' my father has always joked , even telling my serious boyfriends when I brought them home to meet my parents.

It's an interesting situation when you grow up being told that depression runs in your family—especially the women. I'm sure that's why, as a journalist, I've gravitated towards mental health articles, eager to uncover the 'magic' formula to a glass-half-full mentality and discover how some people can look on the bright side while others spend their lives in the shadows.

On a logical level, I know that everyone has blue days, but I've spent my entire life waiting for my inherited depression to catch up with me. Yet it hasn't. In fact, despite facing challenges that would test even the most optimistic person, I would describe myself as a particularly happy person and I think (hope!) that my friends and husband would say the same.

It's important to note here that I don't call myself a naturally happy person. If I'm honest, I don't really believe that naturally happy people exist. In my experience—through my professional work and personal friendship circle—those individuals who remain buoyant, even in the most turbulent waters, are simply better equipped with coping mechanisms to help them to ride the waves rather than sink.

I am a strategically happy person. To counteract my inherited depression and anxiety, I have learnt how to manufacture happiness from coping mechanisms, mental exercises, daily rituals and special people who cast a rose-coloured shine over my environment. In an odd way, I'm grateful that I grew up with a black dog in my living room because, if anything, observing depression at a young age made me more determined to find ways to harness hope, optimism and happiness.

Imagine if you could be happy, regardless?

☐ Regardless of circumstance
☐ Regardless of social status
☐ Regardless of relationships
☐ Regardless of good luck
☐ Regardless of a winning streak

This is the state I aim for. It doesn't mean that I'm invincibly cheerful. I still cry, stagger, stumble, need support and have short periods where sadness overwhelms me for hours or days. But I can always bounce back. I have such a toolkit of happiness-boosting tactics that I can recover from even the most unexpected setbacks and return to my happiness baseline.

Despite experiencing tragedy, loss, disappointments and career misses I always emerge unscathed—or at least still smiling. The happy news? If I can do it when my genetics are predisposed to sadness, than you can too.

☐ DO YOU REMEMBER THE LAST TIME YOU WOKE UP FEELING HAPPY?

This is a question I asked women for an article I wrote about the epidemic of 'low-level sadness' that many people seem to be suffering. Many of the women I interviewed suffered similar symptoms—a general dejection and sense of 'downness' despite the majority having good jobs, close friends and loving partners.

'On the surface I appear content, especially around my colleagues,' one of my case studies confessed. 'But underneath my smile I always default to sadness, particularly when I'm alone, even when I don't really have a reason to be.'

On the back of my article, the newspaper ran a survey asking readers to answer the question: Do you often feel sad? The results were depressing. Nearly 90 percent of respondents answered, 'Yes, I feel down quite a lot' while only 11 percent said they were generally happy.

Interestingly, many of the women I spoke to said they couldn't pinpoint a reason behind their feelings. They weren't ill or jobless; they weren't living in poverty; they had a lot of friends and supportive spouses. Yet they all reported the same sense of despair, joylessness and misery, particularly when they were alone or on waking in the morning.

When I asked them if they could identify when this emotional state began, a lot of women traced it back to an early life trigger—being bullied at school, an unhappy period at home, their first relationship ending badly or finding it hard to fit in at university. During these tough times, sadness had become their default setting. Just like a setting on your smart phone, every time they stopped to recharge themselves their automatic state rebooted to a feeling of dread, despondency and despair.

- Can you relate to feelings of sadness?
- Do you find yourself waking up flat?
- Do you feel down more than up?
- When you rest do you feel dispair?

At this point, it's important to note that some mental health conditions are due to chemical imbalances and you can't just 'think' your way out of them. I'll never forget interviewing the mother of a boy who tried to kill himself at the age of six. Evan suffered from bipolar disorder and he eventually took his life at the age of fifteen by jumping out of his bedroom window. His parents did everything within their power to save him but he was lost in the labyrinth of his mind by then.

When someone close to you suffers from a mental illness, it can be easy to grow frustrated with them and the situation (Why can't they try harder to snap out of it?) But there is big difference to the kind of learned, habitual sadness I'm speaking about and a mental health condition that covers your world in a black shadow.

I would never pretend to be an expert at curing diagnosed conditions like this and can only recommend seeking help from a professional in that area. Over the years, I have recommended that friends ask their doctor for antidepressants and I'm a big advocate of talk therapy (see Chapter 9). But I've also seen the transformative power that you can have over your own psyche.

My friend James Duigan, founder of the Bodyism wellness company and author of an incredible series of books of healthy living once told me, when his dad was dying from cancer: 'I try to remember I'm not an unhappy person. I'm a happy person in a temporarily unhappy situation.' I love this and have fallen back on it during periods when I've been tested. When your default emotion is happiness, it is hard to feel hopeless because beneath the bad days and hard times you know you can find it again.

☐ YOU'LL GET OVER IT EVENTUALLY—MAKE EVENTUALLY TODAY

As a schoolgirl, I had a secret 'memory cleansing' exercise that I would do whenever something bad happened during my day. If a kid teased me or I fell over in the canteen and embarrassed myself, I would blink my eyes hard, just once, and whisper 'gone.' From that moment on, that particular memory would be 'wiped' and I wouldn't be able to revisit it, even if I wanted to.

I was aware, even before puberty, that it was unhealthy to cling to negative events that were in the past and didn't serve me. I was conscious that, because I have such a vivid imagination, I could easily become a 'dweller' and replay a moment over and over again if I didn't find a way to delete it from my mental storage. I blinked away playground bullying, disappointing test results and the time I didn't get to the toilet in time during school assembly. One blink . . . gone!

This wasn't the only secret technique I had to soothe myself when I was younger. I slept with a comfort blanket until I was a teenager (I still have a piece pinned into my hiking backpack for 'emergencies'). As a kid, I loved the ritual of making a 'proper' cup of tea—warming the pot, mixing the tea-leaves and waiting patiently for them to brew, as I watched the steam rise from the kettle and fog the kitchen window. You could say it was my version of a mindfulness meditation.

I also used to spend hours rearranging my mum's sewing kit—lining up spare buttons in rows and winding up balls of wool perfectly. This might sound strange, especially when my friends were playing video games, but I knew these activities calmed me and so I returned to them, over and over, especially if I felt worried, anxious or lonely.

- ○ How do you comfort yourself as an adult?
- ○ How do you self-soothe, in moments of stress or worry?
- ○ How do you ease your own pain or suffering?
- ○ How do you remove unwanted thoughts from your mind?

In hindsight, I have spent my entire life finding ways to cleanse my head, digest toxic thoughts and search for reasons to be grateful. When a baby cries we soothe them, hug them or bring them a favourite toy to play with. But as adults we often just expect to feel better, eventually. Our coping mechanisms are geared towards distraction rather than self-soothing.

I used to drink away my worries but, really, I drunk over them. Some people take drugs, shop 'til they drop, work too much or fill every moment of their social diaries. But these activities only add more to your mind, rather than remove the thoughts and emotions that don't serve you.

- How do you empty your head?
- How do you cleanse your thoughts?
- How do you make space in your mind for positivity to outweigh negativity?

Think about it in terms of personal hygiene. If you feel grubby, you don't just put perfume or deodorant on day after day and hope what's underneath it goes away. You wash away the feeling of discomfort first, because you know that ignoring it will not solve the problem in the long run.

As an adult, I don't 'memory cleanse' in the same way that I did during my childhood, but I have discovered new techniques and coping strategies. If I have a bad day, I gravitate towards the ocean or a swimming pool. I float on my back and imagine black tar running out of my hair into the water. I swish my head from side to side until the 'mental pollution' turns from black to grey and then lilac—my happy colour. When I leave the ocean, I make a conscious decision to leave that toxicity behind me.

I've met a lot of amazing, successful women who have similar tricks. In fact, I learnt the 'tar technique' from entrepreneur Lisa Messenger, the founder of Collective Hub. To cope with stress, she imagines a tap at the base of her spine. When she turns the tap on, black tar runs out of her body and flows away across the ground. She can then walk away feeling lighter and leave her mental 'goo' behind.

It could be as simple as 'shaking it off'—quite literally. When you get up in the morning, stand in your bedroom or your living room and shake your limbs out, fast and furiously, like you're dancing to an upbeat dance track. Shake your arms, shake your legs, shake your hands, shake your feet, then bend over and shake your head upside down.

You may have negativity that has been clinging to your skin for years, from old events, meetings, interactions, tragedy and trauma. Imagine shaking it off like sand, leave it in piles on the floor, dust it off the soles of your feet and walk onwards. We all have a choice about the emotional debris we take forward in this life. It's far harder to move on when you're carrying more than is necessary.

☐ SELF-SOOTHE, SHAMELESSLY

When you're developing your own self-soothing mechanisms, don't worry about how weird, immature, strange or embarrassing they may seem to other people. Don't worry about the coping strategy that is trendy (adult colouring books!), what your best friend does, or even what I've recommended because it works for me. Explore the best ways to sooth yourself, shamelessly. What works might surprise you!

In the last three months of my late husband's life, he suddenly started painting elephants—always elephants—even though he'd never previously shown any interest in art or that animal. In the middle of the night, he'd sit in our sunroom painting with the brightest colours in the palette. Then he'd gift his elephant art to friends and family—the animal that never forgets. My parents still have an elephant in their hallway which they treasure.

On the last day of my husband's life, as his friends and family gathered around his bedside, one of his friends bought a gigantic toy elephant from the hospital gift shop. It was a ridiculous sight—this huge stuffed animal perched on the bed of a 36-year-old man who was unconscious. But in an odd way it soothed everyone in the room, especially me. It certainly broke the ice and every single visitor laughed when they saw it.

The soft toy theme continued afterwards. For months after his death, I carried a giant rabbit-shaped hot water bottle when I left the house, going to the city or visiting friends. It must have been an odd sight—a woman in her twenties sitting on a train with a baby-sized, furry bunny. But at the time it soothed me, calmed me and enabled me to think more evenly. I would fill it with warm water and hold it over my belly—my third chakra—which is where you store fear and trauma.

For a year, I also wore a locket containing my husband's photograph and a lock of hair. It hung on a silver chain around my neck along with a piece of rose quartz—the crystal that heals heartache and love sickness. These props might seem silly to another person but, at the lowest point in my life, they bought me strength, support and comfort. My self-soothing mechanisms might seem immature to some people but they allowed me to find comfort in an uncomfortable situation.

- ◯ What items bring you comfort?
- ◯ What rituals make you calm?
- ◯ Where is the place you can breath?
- ◯ Who are the people you can be yourself with?

Think about your senses—the tastes, smells, sounds, memories and materials that bring you joy and happiness. Then find ways to carry these elements with you during your day, everywhere if needs be.

Even now, I light candles every single evening and burn a specific fragrance of incense—Nag Champa—because it makes my soul glow. I wear floaty clothes made from rainbow fabrics, because they make me feel light and bright. I used to carry a little scent box containing a small piece of sandalwood—a scent that is known to be calming and is often used in meditation. I write in a certain colour of journal—a specific shade of peppermint green—because when I look at it the muscles behind my eyes soften.

I don't know where that elephant is now and the locket is stored away in my pencil case, gathering dust among pencil shavings. That's the thing about self-soothing strategies—at a certain time in your life they can save your sanity but it's also okay to outgrow them.

The Benefits of
A MICRO-MELTDOWN

The secret sobbing session you had in the office bathroom, the meeting where your hands started to shake, the day you just couldn't 'deal' and had to go home an hour early. It's easy to believe that we're the only people who sometimes feel overwhelmed by life and overcome by our feelings.

But you're not alone. In fact, experts say it's better to not have it all together all of the time, and a "micro-meltdown" – momentarily becoming overwhelmed by our emotions – can even work to our advantage.

'There are a lot of benefits to a micro-meltdown,' said psychologist Madonna Hirning, author of the blog Let Me Flourish, who I interviewed for an article on this topic for Collective Hub. 'They can stop people from avoiding difficult feelings, help people to feel more inspired and also, as a leader, make you seem more vulnerable.'

Facebook COO Sheryl Sandberg outed herself as an office crier during a speech at Harvard Business School ("I try to be myself," she said). According to Madonna, emotional meltdowns are more likely to happen at times of transition in a person's life, and we shouldn't fear them.

'It's important to strike a balance between expressing your emotions at work whilst also representing yourself well and taking some ownership of the image you wish to project,' she said. 'You need to engage in self-care and learn from any micro-meltdowns that do occur. Plus, if the meltdowns are becoming a regular occurrence, that may be a sign that you could benefit from professional help to make some adjustments.'

For now, don't feel guilty when you emotionally unravel. Here's how a micro-meltdown can work in your favour.

1. It stops you avoiding difficult feelings

According to the experts, having a micro-meltdown can bring you face-to-face with the very feelings you have been trying to avoid – possibly because you have felt you don't have time to deal with them, or because they bring up thoughts or emotions that you just don't want to have or explore.

'In Western culture – particularly in high-pressured workplaces – the aim and the rewards are focused on appearance; happy, glossy feelings wrapped up in achievement and accolades,' said Madonna. 'We are bombarded with images in our news feeds of what happy and successful people look like and that becomes our comparison point or measuring stick for how we should be.' The result? We avoid 'useful' feelings like sadness or discontentment. 'Dark or uncomfortable feelings can lead to questions we may not want to face but need to,' she said.

'Instead of putting them on the back burner, it brings these feelings to the top – and we can't run away.'

2. You connect with what's important

When we reach meltdown point, we are forced to take notice and assess what is happening in our life. 'The unexpected and usually unwelcome loss of control can come as a shock,' said Madonna. 'However, post-meltdown is a good time to look at the choices and decisions you have been making and the trajectory that these are placing you on.' Think about the lightness you can feel after a good cry, or the freeness you feel after finally confiding in someone. 'You can get the most bang for your buck here if you allow yourself to step back and look objectively at all areas of your life, not just work," she said, 'Assess your level of satisfaction with each and if the degree of time and focus you are placing on each is truly representative of what you most value and how you most want to live.'

3. It releases creative juices

The aftermath of a micro-meltdown can give us a fresh look on life. 'During a meltdown itself you probably won't be thinking too clearly,' said Madonna. 'Your physiology will flood you with stress chemicals that trigger bodily responses such as increased heart rate, sweating and difficulty thinking. However, when the meltdown has subsided and you have re-evaluated the factors, you will likely look at things with a whole new perspective.' This is where the importance of self-cares comes in. Research shows that exercise, meditation and sleep also boost creativity. 'By choosing to value yourself and engage in increased self-care activities, such as connecting with loved ones or space to yourself, you are likely to come back to whatever you were working on with a fresh outlook and new vigour,' she added.

4. You'll be a better leader

A vulnerable leader is more relatable. 'Having a micro-meltdown at work broadcasts to those around us that perhaps we are not the infallible human beings that we try to present as,' said Madonna. 'Before you go into damage control, pause for a minute because all is not lost. The advantages of showing this kind of vulnerability is that it makes you more relatable to others.' Some of the world's greatest leaders are emotionally sensitive – and it makes them more innovative.

'The other unexpected advantage of being vulnerable in front of others is that we are usually more willing to take risks and not play it safe,' she said, 'If you are the high-achieving, image-focused type, it is likely that you are fairly governed by fear. If you are willing to be vulnerable and to lose face in front of others, then taking small risks gets easier – even when you're faced by fear.'

5. It's a learning opportunity

During your lowest moments, there is a lesson to be learnt. 'You can come out of something like this feeling humbled," she said, "The lesson may be simple – you are not bulletproof and you require nurturing and self-care like everyone else. Or it could be more complex. You have new knowledge about yourself and your limitations and what you need and what matters to you." Techniques like meditating or free-writing can help to uncover those lessons, or you may choose to confide in a mentor, life coach or seek therapy. 'You get to freely choose which direction you take from here,' warned Madonna, 'Do you learn nothing and stay on the same path or do you take notice of the learning opportunity that has been presented to you to find choices in your life that, until now, you didn't realise you had?'

FOUR

Breaking Your Rules: Routine vs Ritual

I must have been eight or nine years old when I remember first becoming obsessed with certain repetitive habits. It began with the cushions on the sofa, which I had to line up perfectly straight and without any creases. This may sound like a small thing but I'd spend hours arranging them and rearranging them, straightening then and smoothing them, gripped by a sense of anxiety anytime someone sat on them or changed their position.

I also developed other odd impulses. I read somewhere that a sore neck was a symptom of meningitis and that, if you thought you had the disease, you should check whether you could put your chin on your chest. So I checked—twenty or thirty times a day. Obsessively, compulsively, whenever nobody was looking. And it didn't end there.

For a while, I had to chew every mouthful of food fifteen times. I also had a rule that I had to go to bed at exactly

9.17pm—not a minute more or less. Whenever my dad kissed me goodnight, I had to tell him I loved him eleven times as he walked out of my room, otherwise I was convinced that something bad would happen to him as I slept. If he didn't reply to every 'I love you,' I'd have to start counting again.

'Children crave routine,' my mum has always said and I agree, within reason. According to research, routines and rituals are associated with heightened marital satisfaction and can help children to create a 'sense of personal identity,' as well as improving their academic achievements.[1] But this was different.

It was comforting that we ate porridge every morning as a family, had 'sweetie night' on a Friday, and baked scones together every Sunday before my grandmother visited. However, on top of this, I'd become trapped within a set of secret rules and rituals that were more suffocating than comforting. A professional may have diagnosed obsessive-compulsive disorder (OCD) if I had admitted that I needed help—which I didn't.

In children, common symptoms of OCD include a need for symmetry, a fear of illness and overly sexual thoughts (more on that later). But you don't need to have suffered from OCD to identify with this feeling on some level. Perhaps you've found yourself, in your childhood or adult life, repeating an action, habit or behaviour over and over, even bought it's not only unnecessary but causes you discomfort and anxiety. Do you visit a place repeatedly or engage in an action obsessively, even though you don't really want to and it's actually making your life harder?

I was lucky that I slowly began to push back against these impulses, before they escalated into a real problem. Over time, I learnt to question my habits and also their consequences. When I was gripped by fear for missing a repetition I would ask myself: 'What will really happen if I don't do this thing again?' I tested the consequences: forced myself to crease the cushions and a catastrophe didn't happen; purposefully lost count of my chewing and nobody got hurt.

As a 33-year-old woman, I don't have to tell my husband that I love him eleven times before we go to sleep to avoid disaster. But I'm still, in a sense, that little girl who craves order, symmetry and repetition, especially when life feels chaotic. To the outside world, my life might seem quite unpredictable and spontaneous, but my weeks are scaffolded by routines and rituals that help me to feel stable. The difference is I choose to include these routines and rituals in my world because I want to; they make me feel strong, peaceful and capable.

○ Are you a creature of habit?
○ Does it come from a place of fear or empowerment?
○ Do you rely on these habits because they add to your life?
○ Are you scared that something will be taken away if you don't?

These days, I live my life through conscious choices instead of irresistible urges. But I am still a committed creature of habit. Take my routine now: every morning I drive 45 minutes to the next town to the same cafe, even though there are countless places to buy a cup of tea within walking distance of my house. As soon as I walked into this particular cafe I felt every muscle in my body relax and I smiled. It is part cafe, part bookstore and every day I sit in the same chair and write next to a roaring fire. My words flow and I feel like I've come home. I would drive for six hours every day to harness this feeling. The difference is that, if I can't get to the cafe because my schedule doesn't allow it, I don't feel anxious. I don't need to go there everyday, but I want to.

Over the course of my healing journey I've learnt there is a big difference between the kind of fearful habits that constrained my childhood and the kind of rituals which make you feel calm, capable and cherished.

They say the definition of madness is repeating the same thing over and over, hoping for a different result. But I repeat certain things over and over because I love the result I get from them—happiness!

☐ ALL IN A DAY'S WORK

What's your daily routine? In the past few years, this has become a trendy question to ask in interviews, especially when the interviewee is rich, famous and successful. We know that Anna Wintour plays tennis at 5.45am every day for an hour; Arianna Huffington ignores her smartphone when she first wakes up and instead spends time setting her daily 'intentions'; and former First Lady, Michelle Obama, gets up at 4.30am to swim before her kids wake up and their day begins.

I have to admit I'm a daily routine voyeur. I lap up the details of how other people spend their days—what time they wake up, what they have for breakfast, and the first thought that pops into their heads in the morning. Whenever I ask ambitious types the question, their answer is usually a combination of caffeine, exercise, social media scrolling and breakfast meetings. This is great if it works for you, but I often get the sense that some people's hearts aren't really in it. Do they follow this routine because it makes them wake up sparkling or because Mark Zuckerberg said that's what he does in the morning, so they feel like that's what's expected of them too? In my experience, if you view your morning routine as a chore, then it might be time to change it.

- How do you spend the first hour of your morning?
- How do you celebrate a new day?
- How do you put yourself in the best headspace to enjoy it?
- Do you view your morning as a tick list of items you have to get through?
- Do you feel exhausted just thinking about your schedule?
- When you wake up, do you think, 'Let's get this over with'?

For a long time, my morning routine was more intimidating than invigorating. Throughout my twenties, I thought I was ticking all the right boxes. I woke at dawn every day, went to the gym for a vigorous workout and then cycled forty minutes to my office in all weather conditions. In theory, my morning routine kept me fit, saved me money on public transport and gave me an early endorphin hit that should have set me up to kick all my work goals.

In reality, I arrived at the office utterly exhausted, even before my day had started. I always felt in a rush—flustered, agitated and often angry. I said 'no' to important breakfast meetings which could have furthered my career, because I didn't want to miss my date with the treadmill. I was also thrown into a panic if I heard that bad weather was forecast, because I knew I'd make myself cycle to work in dangerous conditions. On one memorable occasion, I tried to cycle in a blizzard, skidding across a busy highway. Why? It's was just what I did.

When people called me 'dedicated' I took it as a compliment—until I realised that it really wasn't. I'm not saying that we should all go rogue—smash our alarm clocks, eat junk food for breakfast and cancel our gym memberships. But even the healthiest habits can become unhealthy if they are enforced, inflexible and feel more like work than our day jobs. If you go to bed every night dreading your morning routine, it's not empowering; it's debilitating. It's time to question yourself about the alternatives.

I once interviewed Sara Blakely, the founder of Spanx underwear. At the age of 41 she became the world's youngest female self-made billionaire. At that time, she only lived six minutes from her company headquarters but admitted that she purposefully took the longest possible route to work, which often meant driving for over an hour, because it gave her thinking time. She even came up with the name Spanx while sitting at a red traffic light, and was so inspired she had to pull over to the side of the road to write it on a scrap of paper.

I loved this personal insight—not because it's a routine I would like to copy (I am a vomiter in city traffic!) but because it's the perfect example of how morning rituals can be powerful, if you make them personal. Having to endure a long commute is often seen as detrimental to our stress levels, but Sara pushed against this perception. She identified that her commute was actually a window of sacred alone time, when she felt inspired.

These are the kind of morning rituals that I love to hear about—the strange, quirky habits that people have discovered through trial and error; the kind of habits that other people may not understand or relate to. The actress Ellie Kemper, who I interviewed in 2016, describes her morning routine as 'an 86-year-old man's' because she loves getting up before it's light and starting the day with a black coffee. There's a brilliant website called My Morning Routine where people share their daily rituals, from eating breakfast in the nude to 'nature bathing' (spending time in a leafy environment). If checking Facebook makes you feel anxious then avoid it. I know a tech entrepreneur who starts every day by writing code, because it genuinely relaxes him.

My incredible life coach Elli (more on her later) taught me to ask myself one question every morning:

- How do I want to feel today?
- What do I need to do to feel good right now?

Just because your boss starts her day with a green smoothie, it doesn't mean you should too. You don't have to punish yourself at the gym today, just because social media is full of the CrossFit selfies of strangers. What will really leave you feeling energised? I used to worry that if I did this I would fall into a life of vice . . . start each day with a bowl of ice cream and lie in until midday! Trust your intuition—your inner wisdom wants you to be healthy and happy in a way that makes your day feel easy.

These days my routine is a collaborative effort and certainly wouldn't appeal to everyone. Every morning my husband and I both get up at 5am and take a shower together. I do this even when I'm planning to exercise and will soon get sweaty again. We lead such busy lives that our 'co-shower' time is sacred. I wash his hair, he scrubs my back and we chat about our plans and the elements of the day ahead that excite us.

Six days a week I still exercise but I listen to my body. If I feel energised I run hard, if I feel frumpy I dance it off, and if I'm feeling fragile I do yoga on our balcony in the sunshine. Now that I'm pregnant I know my morning routine will soon change again, both during the gestation period and once our daughter meets this earth. In my twenties this would have thrown me into a state of panic, but I'm actually excited to see how our new rituals change and evolve, organically and fluidly.

The rituals and habits you had as a child may not be relevant, practical or empowering now you're a twenty-something student or a thirty-something mother. If that were not the case I'd still be straightening cushions and phoning my dad before bed every night to tell him I love him. Although sometimes I still do that, just because I want to.

□ GOOD NIGHT RITUALS

○ Be a power prepper

What can you do tonight to make tomorrow easier? I learnt this trick from the American personal trainer, Lacey Stone, who I interviewed for an article about the power of evening rituals. Every night she goes to Starbucks and orders a strong, iced coffee, which she keeps in the fridge so that her caffeine hit is ready the next morning. She also lays out her workout kit, packs her gym bags and even plans what she's going to post on Instagram the next morning. 'It might sound quirky but my night prep is vital,' said Lacey. 'The last thing I want to feel first thing in the morning is stressed or rushed. My organisation means I can get out of the door in less than twenty minutes and attack the next day with purpose.'

If you're a night owl whose brainpower peaks in the evening, use this time to be productive and tick something off your to-do list, so that you can wake up the next morning one item lighter.

○ Watch a rerun

Every night as I lie in bed I mentally watch a rerun of my day, like I'm viewing a movie on fast forward. I see myself moving through my day from dawn to dusk: the places I've been to and the interactions and actions that occurred along the way.

I don't overanalyse anything that happened, but I sit back and watch the flow of my day. I look for the moments between the moments: the walk I took from A to B, the winding car drive between meetings, the quiet wait before my husband comes home. It makes me appreciate my day, on a new level, for the sacred moments that are often unappreciated.

○ Don't force it

I used to make myself write in my journal every night before bed, because I read somewhere it would be good for my mental wellbeing. I'm certain this works for some people, but I spend all day writing and by bedtime my creativity is in hibernation. For me, forcing myself to journal before bed became a chore that I dreaded; I looked for excuses to avoid it because it just didn't suit me.

For some people, less is more at bedtime and the most beneficial 'activity' is just to do very little. I once overheard the founder of Twitter, Jack Dorsey, being interviewed by a colleague. When she asked about his bedtime routine he gave a refreshingly honest answer: 'I close my eyes. Isn't that what everyone does?'

FIVE

What's the Rush? Time after Trauma

Now that I'm visibly pregnant, at least three times a week someone looks at my belly and says, 'They grow up so fast!' Every time I hear the sentence, or something similar, a wave of fear sweeps through me, as I have visions of her going to school, leaving home and getting married. One of the side effects of having married a man with only three months to live is that I now live with a constant feeling that time is running out, especially the amount of time I have to spend with my loved ones.

In a good way, this makes me passionate. In a bad way, it can make me clingy. It's hard for my husband to understand why I was in a rush to have a baby or why I struggle to go on a two-day yoga retreat without him. But two days can feel like a dangerously long time to be apart from the man you love, when your first marriage only lasted 28 days before one of you stopped breathing!

You may not have lived through exactly this experience but I don't think I'm the only person to worry about time—or the lack of it. In modern society, time seems to be a concept that many of us struggle with. Although life expectancy has improved dramatically for both sexes in the last century (84.3 years for women according to the Australian Bureau of Statistics), there is still a sense that's not enough. We say things like, 'time is not on our side' and 'there aren't enough hours in the day.' We wake up in a cold sweat worrying about death and a lot of people feel anxious with each passing birthday.

By comparison with our grandparents, there are so many more stages to cram into our life spans. They went to school, got a job, got married and had children. We go to school, go to university, go travelling, get a 'fun' job, get a 'real' job, change careers, sleep around, settle down, save for marriage, then get married. The average age for first-time mothers is getting later and later, as couples feel the pressure to have 'one last big trip' because 'once you have children your time isn't your own.' No pressure!

If you've faced trauma in your early life, time came become even more distorted. A child with separation anxiety will count the minutes until their mother comes to pick them up from the school playground. A three-day wait for a test result can feel like a lifetime if your life depends on it. Yet three months goes by in an instant, when that's your predicted life expectancy.

◯ What does a day in your life mean to you?
◯ How do you value one weekend?

○ How far do you plan ahead?
○ Do you find it difficult to plan more than one month
  ahead?
○ Do you worry that you're falling behind?

All of our unique experiences can give us fear, anxiety, distrust and unease around the passing of time. This can have a positive or negative effect on how we spend, plan and give our time; how we savour or waste it, disregard or seize it.

I've seen people's relationships with time affect their lives in complex ways. A friend of mine, whose older sister died when she was eighteen, refuses to listen to the news and won't discuss worrying topics such as terrorism or global poverty. She is so protective of her time—and ensuring that she is happy all of the time—that she doesn't want to waste a single moment feeling sorrowful. This sounds great in theory, but in reality it's impossible to sustain constant happiness and also closes her off to valuable conversations and experiences.

I have another female friend who plans her free time obsessively. She schedules activities into every weekend in her calendar a year in she, and gets quite upset if people can't commit to dates twelve months in the future. When I asked why he feels the need to plan so far ahead, she told me she believes she is going to die when he is 41 (she's now in her early thirties), despite everyone in her family living to old age. The thought of dying young doesn't scare her, but it does drive his desire to make every weekend extraordinary. Currently single, she only likes to be around people who are fun all of the time and has no tolerance for downtime or boredom.

These are just two examples of how our perception of time can be affected by our personal experiences and influences. Our beliefs around time—that we have too little, that we're too busy, that we need to rush or that something can always wait until tomorrow—can affect our lives in positive and negative ways. They can motivate us to take action, rather than procrastinate. But they can also cause us to move at a pace that isn't sustainable or to live on adrenaline, in a constant fight-or-flight state.

How to savour time:
A JOURNALLING EXERCISE

- ☐ Sit somewhere safe and comfortable with a notebook.
- ☐ Write down your ideal day from start to finish.
- ☐ Use the present tense and only positive verbs.

I wake up in the morning feeling

_____

The first thing I do is

_____

- ☐ Avoid words like 'don't' and 'won't' instead swapping them for positives.
- ☐ Take yourself through every step of your perfect day without overthinking it, including the places you go, the people you meet, the foods you eat and the way you feel. It doesn't have to match your current surroundings. You can wake up in your dream apartment in a different country with a partner who doesn't exist yet if you wish to.
- ☐ Be completely honest and craft a day that makes you feel light, bright and nourished. You might surprise yourself at the perfect day you create.

Now, how can you make that perfect day happen?

☐ TIME TO WASTE

Shortly after I moved in with my husband, a few years ago, my issues with time led to a crisis conversation. The topic arose after a weekend of terrible weather, which meant we had to cancel our plans to go camping and spent the weekend housebound as rain pounded the windows outside and the Met Office circulated a storm warning.

Although my husband is an adventure lover, he is perfectly content to spend all day on the couch watching movies, if rain stops play. I am not! As the day went on, I became increasingly nervous, a balloon of anxiety expanding under my rib cage. By midday, I was itchy with guilt that I should be doing something, anything less ordinary. In the end I went for a run in the middle of a gale, tripped over a fallen branch and returned to our apartment bloody and sobbing. Meanwhile, he continued to sit happily on the couch, peaceful and contented, untouched by the storm swirling around him.

'Why didn't you just stay with me?' he asked.

'Because it's such a waste of a day!' I cried.

As soon as the words left my mouth I realised how bad they sounded.

I was so anxious about stopping, pausing, resting that the thought of spending a quiet day with my boyfriend nearly brought on a panic attack. That's when I knew that I had to think about time differently. I had to stop spending time worrying that it would soon run out, because it was causing me to waste the time I did have.

Part of my problem was that I was letting outside influences dictate when or how I should spend my time. There is so much pressure on all of us, especially in this age of social media. It's the weekend, so you must do something extraordinary; look at what everyone else is doing; what if you don't have a good story to tell on Monday? I was terrified of just having an okay weekend, because that was 48 hours of my life I would never get back again. I believed, as many people do, that weekends must be filled with high-calibre adventures, because from Monday to Friday your focus should be on hard work, grit and productivity.

These beliefs put a ridiculous amount of pressure on my weekends—every weekend—to consist of a montage of unforgettable moments; when actually on some weekends, my body and mind craved the peace and calm of 'extraordinarily ordinary' experiences. If I am truly honest and put my time fears aside for a moment, I love nothing more than waking up on a Saturday, going for a slow walk, stopping at a cafe for a chai tea, then pottering around a market looking at pot plants and knitted beanies. If I put aside my own perceptions and expectations, I could allow myself to enjoy relaxation without guilt—to watch an entire season of a Netflix series back to back, tucked under a warm blanket with my husband with the rain hitting the windows around us.

Since then, I have become less black and white about activities that I see as a waste of time. I'm still not good at relaxing but my husband has found ways to disguise our downtime, so that I'm more comfortable about indulging.

I have a strange phobia around napping in the daytime (this goes back to when I was widowed and found waking up alone hard enough without doing it twice in one day). When my husband knows I'm exhausted, he suggests we watch a documentary—an activity I see as a good use of time—knowing I'll be asleep within ten minutes of the opening credits. On stormy weekends, he'll build a fort in our living room out of bedsheets, chairs and our dining table. We curl up in a double sleeping bag and cook our lunch on a camping stove!

In his book Being Your Self, author Mike George writes: You look at your watch and believe that it is telling you the time! But time is not found on the face of a clock . . . To a being in their natural, timeless awareness, the use of the clock time is just a convenient tool to organise one's attention and energy.

Everybody's attitude to time is affected by their experiences. But it's impossible to waste time, if you spend it carefully and consciously. If you listen to your body and ask yourself: What do I need today? If you are willing to be flexible and malleable, and change your plans to best serve you and the people you hold the closest. Our time management should revolve around what's best for us in the present, rather than our memories from the past or our fears for the future.

During my dad's cancer treatment, he spent 31 days in isolation after a stem cell transplant. During that time, nobody but my mum was allowed to see him for fear of infection. At the start, he said time passed quickly and easily. But towards the end he began to struggle, because his mind kept straying to the future: When will I be let out? When can I go home? He was able to make peace with time when his mind remained in the present, but thinking about the future exacerbated his suffering.

As my belly grows, I have taken my foot off the accelerator of life, both out of want and need. I still have the energy to strive in the mornings and fit my exercise and work into three 'power hours' from 6am until 9am. But the rest of my day is spent slowly and gently. I walk on the beach; I sit on our balcony and draw mind maps; I take my surfboard out in the middle of the day when I know there's not going to be any waves and I can just float around in the shallows.

I would be lying if I said I didn't feel a prickle of guilt sometimes, especially when my husband comes home after an action-packed, ten-hour day at the office. But I've realised that seizing the day comes in many shapes. A day is not wasted if I flow through instead of attacking it. There is no guilt or shame in being able to say your day was easy—in fact there's no better compliment to your timetable. As my pregnancy progresses and people continue to point out that my unborn child's life will 'fly by,' I've adopted a new mantra to rise above my anxiety: Time is always on my side.

☐ THE 'NO RUSH' RULE

My friend Steph, who runs her own PR agency, has been a role model for me when it comes to time management. 'When I used to work for a big corporation I was constantly chasing promotion and achievement, feeling like I was never progressing fast enough,' she says. 'I was so head down and tail up that I missed out on a lot of other opportunities, not just in a career sense but also socially, because I was living on autopilot.'

Although just as ambitious as ever, Steph now has a 'no rush' rule. Rather than worrying about being left behind, she only takes a career step when she feels totally confident to do so. She also moved from fast-paced Sydney to slightly slower Melbourne, because she felt it would help to reset her schedule. 'Funnily enough, I then met my boyfriend in my new city,' she says. 'I previously worried that a relationship would distract me from my career; but I found that when I wasn't in a rush I suddenly had time for everything.'

When I feel like I'm accelerating for the wrong reasons, I write 'no rush rule' on a Post-it note and stick it above my laptop. I am a big believer that new opportunities, whether it's a new job or a new person, can't enter your life if you don't make space for them, energetically. If your train is moving too fast to stop at a station, you don't know what or who you might be missing.

Time:
A CHECKLIST

- ☐ Make time for loving
- ☐ Make time for laughing
- ☐ Make time for resting
- ☐ Make time for being
- ☐ Make time for sitting
- ☐ Make time for staring
- ☐ Make time for healing
- ☐ Make time for dreaming
- ☐ Make time to heal

SIX

When Bad News Happens to Good People

I'll never forget the first moment I found out my father had cancer. I was seventeen and it was the middle of the summer holidays. On that day, I was at a theme park with a group of friends and when my older sister called I was about to step onto a rollercoaster—both physically and emotionally. I remember the landscape spinning as I heard her words, 'Dad's in hospital. He admitted himself. It's Hodgkin's lymphoma.' I vaguely recognised those words from a famous pop star who'd had the illness. 'Is that . . . ?' I asked. 'Yes, it's cancer.'

That was the first time in my adult life that I'd really experienced bad news breaking. As a child, I'd been spoonfed bad news ('Nanny has gone to a better place now'). As a teenager I'd heard the words, 'we need to talk' but never in regard to anything as grave as a life-threatening illness. I can still see myself as if I were a bird flying above the theme park: a seventeen-year-old in a rainbow miniskirt, pushing my way out of the rollercoaster queue and clutching a signpost as my knees buckled. At that age, I'd learnt how to react to bad news by watching soap operas and movies. When faced with tragedy you were meant to cry, collapse and scream. All of which I did. None of which was helpful.

When was the last time you got bad news?

How did you react to it?

When I talk about bad news, it doesn't need to be as over-powering as a cancer diagnosis or a terminal prognosis. It could be in the form of a work disappointment, a rejection letter, a redundancy, a parking ticket or those ten stinging words: 'I love you but I'm not in love with you.' You can probably pinpoint exactly where you were when the bad news broke; who you were with, what you were wearing, the smells, sounds or tastes surrounding you.

We can even do it about bad news that's not directly related to us. Can you remember exactly where you were when Princess Diana died? When the planes hit the Twin Towers? When the tsunami hit Indonesia?

In psychology, they use the acronym SARA to describe how people react to news they're not expecting: Shock or Surprise, Anger or Anxiety. Rejection or Rationalisation and finally Acceptance. It's a healthy, healing cycle when you move through it successfully. The problem arises when people get stuck on one phase such as anger, then exist in that emotion for weeks, months, years—even a lifetime. We say things like the news paralysed me and I froze to describe the shock and resulting sense of stuckness it causes.

After my dad got sick and then my husband died, my mum developed a crippling phobia of the telephone. It might sound like a small eccentricity, but it became a debilitating problem. She refused to answer the phone if nobody else was home, because she was terrified that it would be someone delivering bad news to her. Years later, she was still being affected by a piece of bad news from the past, even after my father was in remission.

When faced with bad news, it can be easy to react on autopilot. Perhaps, like my seventeen-year-old self, you've been conditioned by popular culture to react in a certain way. When a partner breaks up with you, buy a tub of ice cream and tear up his photographs! Didn't get that promotion? Make a scene and storm out of the office. But is any of that behaviour actually going to make you feel better? Or are you just going to end up adding to your emotional turmoil?

That day at the theme park wasn't my last brush with bad news. Two years later, I was walking home from university when my sister phoned to say Dad had relapsed and been paralysed from the waist down, because a tumour had grown around his spinal cord. A few years after that, a doctor in a Dublin hospital asked me to follow him into a tiny room where he informed me that my fiancé would probably be dead within three months. I'd just been to the hospital canteen and was carrying a soft-scoop ice cream which melted over my fingers.

On both of these occasions, I reacted differently to the first time. By this point, I'd learnt that over-the-top dramatics didn't serve me. My coping mechanisms had evolved and

I'd discovered ways to react, process and adapt to each new reality more quickly. In the case of my husband, I remember walking to the elevator foyer and calling my dad to tell him. I then called my sister and asked if I could stay with her after his death. I went back to the oncology ward and sat with my fiancé for two hours without mentioning it, as he chatted about a wedding we were planning twelve months away.

On our drive home I took a detour, stopping at a secluded harbour on the edge of the ocean. That is where I became the breaker rather than the taker of bad news, telling the man I loved that his doctors believed his life would soon be over. I cried but he didn't. Instead he turned to me and smiled. 'They're welcome to their opinion' he said, 'but I don't believe them. I know I'm going to beat this.' He didn't, but that doesn't matter. All that mattered was that in that moment he believed it. When faced with arguably the worst news a person can receive he chose his own reaction and, by doing so, was able to control the explosion.

☐ DAMAGE CONTROL

I would never tell anyone how they should react to bad news, but I have learnt that you can choose how to react in most situations. You can choose peace. You can choose to contain the trauma, even at a time when your reality is shattering. You can ignore the experts if you want to, and if it helps you. You can stay standing rather than falling to your knees, or you can lie down on the floor very silent and very still if it soothes you.

When one of my incredible friends, Nat Kringoudis, a Chinese medicine practitioner and fertility specialist, found out her newborn son had cystic fibrosis she was devastated but knew she needed to digest her heartbreak quickly, so she would be capable of caring for him. She sent all her friends and family members a group email, explaining what had happened but asking that none of them call her until she got in touch with them. Then she went into a 'grieving pit' for three days, shutting herself in her house with no contact with the outside world. 'As a Chinese medicine practitioner, I've done a lot of research into the grief process,' said Nat,. 'I've read studies that suggest grief can take just 72 hours, if you totally immerse yourself in your feelings. I had to feel the pain and avoid distractions.' It wouldn't work for everyone but it did for her. She gave herself permission to feel her grief intensely, then decided to let those feelings go. And they did.

Many of us live in fear of bad news—both giving it and receiving it. The reality is that few of us will escape bad news in our personal or professional lives, but it doesn't have to destroy you or overshadow all the good news in your life. Taking bad news in your stride doesn't mean you're in denial.

When I was writing this chapter, I found a journal that I wrote around the time my first husband got sick. On the day his cancer was diagnosed, 24th October, I wrote a checklist of how I wanted to react to his illness:

☐ Don't question him about things he can't yet answer.
☐ Start the day on a positive note and the rest will follow.

- ☐ Don't let depression become the norm—remember it's your choice to mourn.
- ☐ Handle your grief with the grace of a woman, not the grief of a child.
- ☐ Remember that you're still the same person. This isn't your disease.
- ☐ Remind him why he loves you every day. Make him smile every day.
- ☐ Don't become a victim. You're far too young to accept this as your lot.
- ☐ Come out stronger!!!

I didn't always achieve all of those aims (I'm only human after all) but it did help me to try. Over the next eight months, in between his diagnosis and death, we were able to have a happy life. In between doctors' appointments, chemo sessions and scans that showed the cancer was spreading, we allowed ourselves to laugh, smile and continue to plan a life together.

These days, whenever I receive bad news I try to pause, even for a second, before reacting. Then I'm guided by my intuition. This could mean asking for more information so I can understand someone else's decision, giving myself space to process quietly, or screaming into a cushion (an exercise my life coach recommends to release emotion).

I was once sent to interview the victim of a shark attack, who had been mauled by a three-metre bull shark while he was surfing. Although his circumstances were uncommon— in the past 50 years there have been only 47 unprovoked shark attack fatalities in Australia—the emotional side effects were amazingly familiar: insomnia, self-doubt, social withdrawal, and a tendency to become overemotional when triggered. At the time, my closest girlfriend was going through a break-up and was experiencing the same symptoms as she tried to process what had happened to her.

After his attack Dave created the support group, Bite Club, to connect other victims and their families. He discovered that many shark attack survivors suffer from post-traumatic stress disorder (PTSD), slide into alcoholism or drug dependency. But Dave is one of the exceptions. He spoke about his experience with absolute acceptance, peace and optimism. So, what was his secret?

'I put the attack into perspective with the rest of my life,' he said. 'Some years ago, I lost a child at nine and a half months, which destroyed my marriage. My father was crushed by a forklift truck. My brother is also disabled. It's those things that I look back on and draw strength from. By comparison, this is just an injury.' Dave even still surfs in the spot where he was attacked. The first time back, he sat on his board and spoke to the ocean. 'Let's move on from this,' he recalls saying. He added, 'It was a magical moment.'

Imagine if we could all make peace with the dark water that has swallowed us up in the past. If we could all face a personal attack with such grace, even when we didn't see it coming.

A Vedic meditation teacher once told me that living consciously isn't about wishing yourself out of a tough situation. It's about setting an intention as to how you want to react in it. That doesn't mean everyday challenges don't affect me. I still get nervous before big work meetings.

I still cry when faced with confrontation. But I try not to exaggerate my reactions or drag them on unnecessarily. If I cry its because I truly need to release an emotion, rather than because I think it's the 'expected' thing to do in that situation.

When bad news breaks, who do you want to be? When I'm faced with bad news, I want to be able to look back on the moment and feel proud of myself. Amidst the shock, outrage, and fear, you can still remain true to yourself, rather than acting the part of a spurned lover, a disgruntled worker, a widow.

For me, this also applies to physical reminders you hold onto after a tragedy. I don't think there's anything wrong with keeping souvenirs from the toughest points in your life. We collect trinkets, reminders and souvenirs from all the positive and memorable milestones in our lives, so it makes sense to do the same for events at the other end of the spectrum. But I do think it's important to be conscious about where you keep your stash of survivor souvenirs and how often you dip into them.

For a time, it may help you to have constant reminders of your past around you—a jumper belonging to your ex, a necklace that was a gift from a friend, a business card from your old job in your wallet. It's fine to carry these things with you (remember my giant rabbit!) if they genuinely bring you comfort. But be open to the fact that one day it will be time to store them—and don't feel guilty for doing so.

In my garage, I have a memory box of items that belonged to my first husband—his favourite T-shirt, his passport and mobile phone that still holds our final text messages. I would never throw it away but I also don't feel the need to pore over it, even on anniversaries of our relationship.

I wore my wedding ring for years after my husband died. In the early days I couldn't imagine ever taking it off, but that feeling didn't last forever. I found myself finding an excuse to take it off—because I was going swimming, because I was doing the washing up, because I was eating a sandwich and it might get messy.

One day during a session with my psychotherapist I admitted that I hated wearing it. She asked me to take it off and an incredible thing happened: my shoulders instantly relaxed. The physical affect was visible and so dramatic both our eyes widened. She told me to put it back on and my shoulders tightened and shot upwards. We repeated it over and over, both amazed by the impact of this innocent accessory.

I never wore that wedding ring again.

☐ THE CRISIS COMEDOWN

There is a side effect of bad news that people don't often talk about—the strange comedown that can happen in the weeks or months afterwards. You might have experienced it yourself after everyone else's lives have returned to normal: your friends stop calling every day, your boss asks when you're coming back to work and no-one leaves lasagne on your doorstep anymore.

After an unexpected event there is a period of grace where normal life is suspended; you're the centre of attention and all rules go out the window. It can manifest in mysterious ways. The night my husband died I remember sitting in the nurses' station with a cup of tea and a packet of biscuits, after they rolled his body to the morgue. I was in mourning but it crossed my mind—quite joyfully—that I could eat a third chocolate biscuit without feeling guilty. If you can't eat chocolate when your husband has just died, when can you?

Even if you've never experienced a personal tragedy, you may have found yourself seduced by the thought of disaster. Have you ever fantasised about a terrible event turning your life upside down? A car crash that brings your friends rushing to the hospital, an illness that fixes your relationship, or a freak natural disaster hitting your city? It's a clichéd Hollywood storyline—the guy only admits he loves the girl after she has been kidnapped or involved in a near-death experience.

You can get hooked on a feeling of living in a heightened state of crisis. There's even a term for it—chaos addiction. According to psychologist, Dr. Keith Lee, people are 'increasingly seduced into believing that intensity equals being alive.[1]' You think you want life to return to normal but when it does, to your surprise, you miss the thrill that comes from existing in a soap opera. This means that, even when a crisis naturally passes, you can find yourself looking for a way to extend it—or even create a new one.

One of my girlfriends regularly imagines her own funeral; who would come, who would read her obituary and what they would say about her. It's not that she wants to die but she is curious about the butterfly effect of her exit. She also fantasises about being in a freak accident, just bad enough to put her in hospital for a short period so she can take time off work without feeling guilty.

I suffered from this in the past, especially when I was younger. When I was a teenager, I was under the illusion that drama made you more popular. The coolest girl in my secondary school had scars all down her arm and a notebook full of dark poetry and doodles of stick figures hanging themselves. When I was coming of age it wasn't very cool to be happy—fashion magazines were full of dark eyeliner and 'heroin chic' supermodels. I faked pregnancy scares to get my boyfriend's attention. When I was seventeen, I took a cheese grater to my forehead and told my boyfriend that I'd been attacked in a dark alley. My eating disorder relapsed after my dad went into remission, when life returned to some semblance of 'boring' normality.

We need to start talking about the comedown that can come after a crisis and the strange sense of loss that can occur when a bad patch passes. When you're 'out of the woods' and the worst is behind you, self-sabotaging behaviour can emerge and the real damage can be done.

☐ HOW TO WORRY IN THE RIGHT WAY

◌ Contain your concerns

Do you ever feel your worries are overwhelming you? Does anxiety intrude into your day uninvited, when you're trying to watch a movie or celebrate a friend's birthday? Some people have an amazing ability to only worry at relevant moments, to only think about work when they're at the office or worry about test results when they're in a doctor's waiting room. It's an ability we can all practise.

Researchers at Penn State University found that coming up with a time and place to think about a worry can help to contain it.[1] Instead of letting negativity cloud your entire day schedule a 'worry window'—it could be thirty minutes in the morning, when you sit down with a notebook and write down everything that is concerning you. The study made use of a technique, called 'stimulus control.' By compartmentalizing worry — setting aside a specific half-hour period each day to think about worries and consider solutions, and also deliberately avoiding thinking about those issues the rest of the day — people can ultimately help reduce those worries, research has shown.

I've heard a similar strategy can help with grief. Try setting aside fifteen minutes every week (or every day if you need it), where you sit down in a safe place and surrender to heartbreak. At the end of the fifteen minutes, imagine a glowing ball of white light in your heart that grows and fills your entire body, from the centre of your heart to your fingers and toes. Imagine it shining out of your skin into the room, filling it from wall to wall and shining out of the windows. Then let your grief go until your next date with heartbreak.

◯ Don't keep calm

Worried about an event or an important work meeting? A study by researchers at Harvard University found that, when participants were asked to speak publicly or sing in front of a crowd, those who were told to be excited performed better than those participants told to keep calm[1]. The theory is that, physiologically, it is easier for our bodies to move from anxiety to excitement than from anxiety to calmness, as the latter is too much of an opposing emotion. When you're worried about something, it can seem hard to find a reason to be excited, so try this: be excited that the event you're dreading will soon be over. As you lie in bed on the morning of the event you're worried about, imagine how you will feel lying in bed that evening when it's all behind you. Allow yourself to feel excited about the moment when your relieved head will hit the pillow.

○ **Imagine a happy ending**
Are you prone to catastrophise? Do your worries infiltrate your dreams? Do you play out unfortunate events in your head before they happen? A four-step process called Imagery Rehearsal Therapy is often used to treat people suffering from recurring nightmares:

Step 1: Write down as much of your dream or daydream as you remember, including intimate details.

Step 2: Write down a more positive ending to the story.

Step 3: Rehearse this new ending in your mind every night before going to sleep, to rest your thought process.

Step 4: Practise a relaxing breathing exercise to calm your nervous system. Repeat the exercise though the day, on the train, in the shower or in the elevator up to your office. Nobody need even know.

SEVEN

Art Ache: The Power of Creativity

When I was a little girl, whenever I walked to school with my mum I used to imagine a narrator telling the story of my life, as if I were a book character:

> As Amy walked along the road, she took her mum's hand and squeezed it tightly. She stopped to tie up her shoelace. She had worn her lucky socks that day to help her with her maths test.

Even when I felt scared or fearful, my inner narrator would always find a reason to be grateful:

> Amy hoped that she could remember her times tables. But as the sun shone on her face, she was excited about playing outside at lunchtime.

It might sound odd to have a storybook narrator as an imaginary friend but I discovered at a young age that, by observing my life as an outsider, I could put distance between myself and a worrying situation.

This is not the only way that I used my imagination to self-soothe during my childhood. From an early age I discovered that creativity—particularly expressing my emotions on paper—could help me to deal with unsettling feelings, anxiety, loneliness, guilt or sadness. As a book lover, I would immerse myself in imaginary worlds, listening to Roald Dahl cassette tapes before bed to relax and distract myself. As I listened to the stories being read aloud, I'd imagine how I'd transform the book into a theatre production—the sets, the costumes, the characters, where the actors would stand and how the audience would react.

When I was naughty and my mum sent me to my bedroom, I would ease my punishment by writing poetry. When my mum came up to release me from quarantine, I would say to her, 'I'm busy.' I was so engrossed in a project that I didn't want to go downstairs, even when I was allowed to.

Over the years, creativity has helped me to heal myself, observe myself and discover my hangs-ups and sore points. At the height of my anorexia when I was seventeen, I enrolled in an art college. My end-of-year project was a series of self-portrait photographs, in which I pretended to slit my wrists and 'bleed' fluorescent paint over the floor of a warehouse. The following year, when I specialised in fashion, I designed a dress made of peacock feathers (the attention-seeking bird) that was threaded with torn up photos of my family. Analyse that!

The healing benefits of creativity are being increasingly proven. Whether it's art, music, writing or dancing, creative expression has been shown to make us happier and healthier. It can decrease negative emotions and increase positive ones, improve medical outcomes, help people to express grief and improve their self-identity.[1]

When we are creative or engage in activities that require imagination and improvisation, we are in 'flow'—a state of heightened focus and immersion in activities such as art, play and work. Positive psychologist Mihaly Csikszentmihalyi, who pioneered the exploration of creativity flow, describes it as a form of ecstasy.[1] The word 'ecstasy' in Greek means simply to stand to the side of something. So, ecstasy is essential for stepping into an alternative reality in which you can leave your worries behind, even momentarily.

Art therapy is open to everybody, even if the only thing you've ever painted is your bedroom walls. In fact, you may already be doing it without realising eg.

☐ The book you read in the bath.
☐ The picture you doodle in a meeting.
☐ The song you hum in the shower.
☐ The dress you wear to cheer yourself up.
☐ The cake you bake on a rainy day.
☐ The way you wrap a friend's birthday present.
☐ The improvisation you do in yoga.

These are all examples of creative actions that, on some level, can change your mental state for the better. I interviewed a young mother who took up pottery to recovery from post-traumatic stress disorder caused by a traumatic labour (now she sells her work on Etsy). As part of another article, I profiled a 'surf doodler' who began drawing line illustrations of waves as a form of meditation, to relieve stress after he emigrated to a different country.

I interviewed a comic book illustrator who created a comic book about mental illness. The main character, Lana, crumbles into shards of glass whenever she has a panic attack (she later learns to use it as a superpower). In an article about entrepreneurs inspired by grief, I included Alyssa Monks, an artist who processed the death of her mother by taking her canvas into a forest and painting wild, untamed landscapes.

Most memorably, I spent a day at the children's hospice Bear Cottage, speaking to their art therapist about how they use creativity to help terminally-ill children and their carers. The week before my visit, they hosted a group of mums who'd all lost babies less than a year old. They hung huge white bedsheets on the walls in the garden and the mums threw tins of paint at the canvases.

There is a misconception that to be creative—and reap the benefits—you need to be able to create something worthy of a gallery. But you don't need to be an artist to have a creative outlet. In her book, Creativity to Reinvent Your Life, one of my favourite spiritual authors, Miriam Subirana, says that creativity is a gift that each of us has which can take us 'from pain to wellbeing, from separation to union, from repression to expression, and from loneliness to creative solitude.'

This can include thinking creatively at work or finding creative ways to solve a problem you see in your life or the wider world around you. One of my husband's creative outlets is recycling, because he says he likes thinking of inventive ways to repurpose or rethink uses for objects. Recently, I interviewed the model and activist Olly Henderson who, at Australian Fashion Week in 2013, hand-painted a hundred T-shirts with social slogans proclaiming Sexism Sucks, Reject Racism and Homeless are Human. Her social enterprise, Start to Riot, now collaborates with artists, dancers and musicians to engage young people in issues that matter, from sexual violence to gender inequality and global warming.

To me, creativity is all about releasing energy, like a plume of smoke rising from a manhole in New York City. Creativity can give us a new perspective, open our eyes to new experiences, enable us to reinvent ourselves and find a voice. Creativity shows up in how we walk, how we talk, how we dress and how we choose to wash our hair in the shower. Creativity is so much more than just art. It is how we frame our story; how we choose to present it to ourselves and to the world.

☐ THE DIFFERENCE BETWEEN SURVIVING AND THRIVING IS IMAGINATION

You may know the story of Turia Pitt, the Australian marathon runner who was trapped in a bushfire during a 100km race through the outback, suffering burns to 65 percent of her body. Known as the 'girl in the mask' because of the protective covering she had to wear over her facial burns, doctors warned Turia that she might never talk or walk again. Yet she made a miraculous recovery, through the power of determination and imagination. A few years ago, I was lucky enough to interview her.

'When I was in hospital, covered head to toe with bandages, I would imagine that I was an SAS soldier who'd been blown up on patrol in Afghanistan,' said Turia. 'By perceiving myself as that bloke who was hard as nails, I immediately started to toughen up.' It was a strategy she had learnt as an athlete when, during swimming training, she would imagine that a shark was chasing her to make her go faster.

More than just a survivor—and certainly not a victim—Turia has since then hiked the Kokoda Track and completed her first ironwoman competition, swimming 3.8km, cycling 180km and running 42.2km in just over 13 hours. She's not the only person to use visualisation techniques to allow her to heal, deal and process her feelings.

Seeing yourself completing a goal can take you one step closer to achieving it, especially at the lowest points in your life. It could be a personal aim (getting married, falling pregnant), reaching a professional milestone or a fitness achievement. I've interviewed professional athletes, entrepreneurs, musicians and scientists who all imagined their breakthrough moment over and over again, long before it actually happened, whether it was visualising themselves crossing a finishing line, looking through a microscope or stepping onto the stage of a packed-out stadium.

When you visualise where you want to be, you don't need to know how you're going to get there. More than a decade before Sara Blakely appeared on the Oprah Winfrey show to promote her now-famous underwear brand, she used to imagine sitting on the talk show host's couch. In her visualisation, she didn't know what they'd be talking about ('I knew I'd fill in the blanks later').

In her earlier life, the entrepreneur also used creative visioning to overcome trauma, after she witnessed her best friend being hit and killed by a car at the age of sixteen. To cope, she began listening to self-help tapes by Wayne Dyer, including How to Be a No-Limit Person which teaches techniques for greeting each day with high expectations and a clear sense of direction. 'It was so impactful to me at that point in my life, when I was down and needed support,' says Sara. 'I learnt the power of positive thinking and started believing in myself and manifesting my future.'

Visualisation can even help us to deal with illness, as I learnt when I met Amelia Hill, a 38-year-old woman who suffers from a condition called multiple chemical sensitivity. This means she is intolerant to an endless list of everyday items, including fragrances, fabrics, plastics, cleaning products and even electricity. Her symptoms began at the age of fifteen, when she first experienced shortness of breath and exhaustion, and became more severe as she got older.

Her condition is now so severe that, for long periods of the year, Amelia has to live in a 'safe room' in her house, with visitors speaking to her through a glass window. 'My old life as a fashion stylist seems like a distant memory,' she said. 'I used to spend my days surrounded by beauty, colour and fabulousness. There were days when giving up seemed like an option.'

As Amelia's condition improved and she was able to use a computer for short periods, she found imaginative ways to keep looking forward through meditation and positive visualisation. One of those techniques is the hashtag #FutureSelfFriday. On Facebook, she posts imaginary status updates of where she hopes to be in the future. 'In New York, going to walk my favourite stretch of Central Park, drinking in the soft dappled light and the breeze.' She even imagines her future relationships. 'I've always been a hopeless romantic, so my future self also has a hot husband,' said Amelia. 'While I am a realist and know they may never find a cure, I also haven't given up on my fairytale ending.'

There are no rules to creative healing and the process is extremely personal. You might choose to take up an art class, to plant a fruit and vegetable garden (mine has taught me a lot about recreation and patience) or start a #5yearsfromnow Instagram account depicting your dream life five years from now.

I've heard people say, 'I can't imagine ever being happy again.' What they really mean is: I can't imagine being happy in exactly the same way I was before. A creative mindset can help you to rethink your path to happiness and reinvent your new reality as a dazzling work of art.

☐ CRAFTING YOUR FUTURE

As my my due date approaches, I'm currently spending a lot of time imagining my ideal birth: the look on my husband's face when he holds his daughter; the look on my mother's face when I introduce her to her first grandchild; how we plan to transform the hospital delivery room into a happy, hippy sanctuary with colourful sarongs, cushions and aromatherapy oils.

You could say I'm setting myself up for disappointment by imagining the perfect drug-free delivery. I know that when it comes to delivering a baby, the best-laid plans can go out the window and the peaceful, natural delivery I'm envisioning could turn into an emergency. But rather than focus on the worst-case scenario, I would rather use my energy to prepare for the best outcome.

In a sense, I even used visioning to conceive our miracle baby. When my husband and I were trying to fall pregnant, I suffered moments of intense self-doubt. I didn't have a period for seven years after my first husband died. My last period was on the day of his funeral and they only returned a week after I met my current husband, the future father of my baby—how incredibly insightful is the female body?

It didn't take us long to conceive but it felt like a lifetime. I was so worried that, because of my history, I wouldn't be able to fall pregnant at all. We heard that close friends were having a baby the day after I'd done a negative pregnancy test. I took myself for a hike, sat in the middle of a forest trail and sobbed until my body felt empty. I felt so sure there was a baby's energy around us, but I didn't know if my body was capable of a welcome.

I could have let negativity absorb me (and I did on some days). But instead, I used creativity as a conception tool. One night, after a pregnancy test came back negative, I sat down at my laptop and created a vision board from images I found on Pinterest and Google. I created an image of the ideal life I wanted to lead as a family of three. A surfer walking to the beach with a tiny toddler. A writer typing at a computer with a baby in a sling across her chest. A little blonde girl sitting in a tent staring out across a mountain valley.

I only chose photographs that resonated deeply within me, instantly. After collating the pictures, I set it as the screensaver on my computer, my iPad and iPhone, so that I couldn't avoid it. At the centre of the collage, I positioned the picture that made my heart glow– a pregnant bride cradling her bump on her wedding day.

I looked at that photo every day and imagined the joy she must be feeling, committing to the man that she loves as a new life grows inside her. As my wedding day approached—with still no baby—I kept staring at my vision board and never stopped hoping. Two days before our big day, a pregnancy test came back positive. At 5pm on the night before our wedding, our doctor phoned with the result of a blood test. Now, whenever I look at photos of our ceremony I smile, knowing we had a secret wedding guest.

Whenever a friend is feeling lost or hopeless in her life, I recommend vision boarding. Whether it's cutting and sticking pages from a magazine or saving and pinning them from the internet, it's an amazing exercise to help you to manifest your dream future. However, this doesn't mean you can then sit back and do nothing.

A friend once asked me, 'How long will it take to come true?' after we'd put together her vision board one afternoon. It's not an instant fix that will magically make you wake up in an alternate life. But it will give you clarity, motivation, focus and inspiration to move your life in a certain direction.

Although the centre point of my vision board did come true and I stepped into the shoes of that pregnant bride, there are still images surrounding it that haven't come to fruition . . . yet. I don't have a pile of children's books that I've written. We don't own a forest retreat. I don't make surfing look easy. But the montage of my 'ideal' life that I've cut and pasted make me smile because it holds such magical potential. Sometimes, for now, it's enough to see a dream, even when you can't step into the picture just yet.

☐ HOW TO WRITE AWAY YOUR WORRIES

If you're in my inner circle (a friend, a relative or a colleague), at some point in our relationship I will probably give you a journal as a present. Keeping a journal has been shown to reduce anxiety, promote mindfulness, boost memory and empathy and even improve your relationships, because you're practising your skills of communication.

I have kept a journal since I was a schoolgirl and I'm in good company. Oprah, Arianna Huffington and Tim Ferriss are all fans of journalling. The founder of Twitter, Jack Dorsey, uses the Day One Journal app, to digitally note down his thoughts on a daily basis.

You might think you're not a writer but everyone who can string more than two words together is. The best thing about the therapeutic journalling retreats I run is seeing people who haven't written anything more personal than a work report since school so absorbed in their journalling— in the flow of creativity. You can see their disappointment when I call time on an exercise.

The best thing about journalling as a form of therapy is that it's accessible to everyone, can fit into your life easily, and doesn't cost more than the price of a pen and a notebook. The hardest part is turning to page one and getting started.

Here are my top tips for journalling:

○ **Forget political correctness**
Whether or not you call yourself a writer, I recommend that everyone reads the book Zen in the Art of Writing by Ray Bradbury. In it he talks about the power of writing without censoring yourself. 'How long has it been since you wrote a story where your real love or real hatred somehow got onto the paper?' he says. 'When was the last time you dared to write a cherished prejudice so it slammed the page like a lightning bolt?'

In this era of social media especially, we constantly edit and filter ourselves so that we don't offend friends, lose followers or give strangers a bad impression of us. This is natural, but your journal is not a place to censor yourself or write about a 'safe' subject. At my journalling retreats, we always do an exercise from Zen in the Art of Writing. Split your notebook into three columns labelled Love, Hate and Fear. Then spend ten minutes listing things you that associate with those words. Those words become your writing prompts. Whenever you feel like you need to emotionally release something but you can't pinpoint exactly what, choose a word from the lists and journal about it for fifteen minutes—uncensored. You might be surprised what comes up.

⌒ Buy stationary that sings to you

I am very particular about the journals I write in and the pens I use to write with. I spoke before about the fact that I always write in a peppermint-coloured journal, but that's not where my pickiness ends. I always write in blue biro—never black—and I use orange and grass-green pencils to highlight words or sentences that I want to emphasise. This might seem odd, but when I'm writing these elements help me to relax and feel calm and comfortable. I think of it as interior decoration. I am setting up a safe space where I can create. It's no different than choosing to journal in my favourite chair with the window blinds open just enough to let the perfect amount of light in.

Remember how much care you would take choosing a pencil case as a child? That's how much care you should take when choosing your journalling apparatus. Spend an hour at a stationary shop browsing, testing, holding options until you know—this is it! The yoga teacher I run my retreats with uses a journal with a dinosaur on the front saying 'Roar!' and also writes in bright pink pen. She says it makes her smile whenever she looks at it.

⌒ Remember you're not at school

Forget proper grammar, spelling mistakes and coherent sentences. Your journal is not a space for judgement or criticism. It is a place where you can cross out words, leave out letters and smudge ink across the paper with reckless abandonment, because it really doesn't matter. Some people find this easier than others. I've taught journalling techniques to lawyers, accountants, teachers and scientists who are professional perfectionists so often squirm when I encourage them to let their mistakes go.

When you relax into your writing and your flow, your attention to detail might waver. But that's just a sign you're delving emotionally deeper. In the past six months of his life, I encouraged my first husband to keep a journal. It got progressively messier, more illegible and chaotic, but that didn't matter. You can feel the raw emotion erupting from the paper.

○ **Promise yourself no-one will read it**

As humans, we are born performers and seek praise and reassurance. That's perfectly fine! But the biggest enemy of creativity is self-consciousness. On my journalling retreat, I tell people to spend two minutes answering the question: Who am I? I warn them that at the end of the exercise we will all share our answers aloud. We don't! I just want them to see how fear of judgement affects their writing. We then repeat the exercise knowing that nobody will ever read their answers. It's incredible to see how differently we create when we know that our work will be on show afterwards.

It can take time to trust yourself when you're journalling—to trust that you're not going to read what you've written to anyone else, feel the need to analyse it with anyone else or call your mum to read her your amazing revelation. But you have to promise your subconscious that no matter what you write—whether good or bad, happy or sad—you won't share it. The whole point of journalling is to give yourself permission to express the thoughts you dare not say aloud.

◌ Create a safe space

Some people seek isolation and silence when they're writing, while others need the energy of noise and the buzz of other people. I fall into the second category. My favourite place to journal is a busy cafe with a pot of milky chai tea sweetened with honey. I always take off my shoes and sit crossed-legged, preferably on a long bench so I have lots of space to get comfortable. If I'm writing about a topic that's sensitive, I put a cushion over my belly because it brings me comfort. I wear my hair down because it makes me feel softer and more vulnerable, in a good way. I am happy for strangers to come and join my table. In fact I welcome them, because I've found the energy of other people helps me to be creative.

You may find you crave the opposite—absolute silence and total solitude—and that's perfect too. Either way, explore the environment that make you feel safest and then give yourself permission to seek out that atmosphere or replicate it as much as possible.

When my husband and I were backpacking across South America, one of my magical moments was spent journalling in a busy market in Peru, sitting at a wooden table next to an old lady selling hot chicha morada—a local drink made from purple corn and condensed milk. I took off my shoes, crossed my legs, let my hair down and pulled out my blue biro. I was in the middle of a strange new country but felt like I'd come home.

EIGHT

Are You Too Good for Your Own Good?

Every few months, I meet up with an old friend and our catch-ups follow the same pattern. Now in her thirties, she tends to crash from one career crisis to another, so inevitably will have just quit one job and be searching for her next one. She'll arrive late, minus her wallet, meaning that she won't be able to pay for lunch. At some point during the meal, she will say something along the lines of, 'You're so lucky, Amy. You have it all.' She envies my career, my salary and my prospects. But the truth is, I envy the chaos she inhabits: her ability to be gloriously unproductive and non-strategic, living hand to mouth and coasting from one career to another.

From a young age, my drive to succeed has been overpowering and my ambition abounding. In a good way, it has enabled me to survive in a (very!) competitive industry but I've also discovered that being overly ambitious can be tortuous. If not managed correctly, it can be isolating, exhausting and soul-destroying. You can lose weekends, holidays, friends, loves and hobbies. If you're not careful, you can lose your sense of self.

A few years ago when I was in my late twenties, I wrote an article for the Daily Mail about this downside of being a high achiever. You might remember the story because, to my surprise, it went viral. This was mainly because of this one sentence in the piece: I wish that I could be as mediocre as my friends. In a single week I had tens of thousands of Tweets, Facebook messages and emails, plus invitations to appear on every current affairs television show in Australia.

I've written hundreds of articles during my career but this one caused the biggest stir—and was the most divisive. People who contacted me were either passionately for or against me. The trolls called me arrogant, conceited and a lot of other names that I can't write in print. But their hatred was balanced out by an abundance of emails from people—largely women—who contacted me privately to say, 'I feel like this too!'

Perhaps you've experienced the downside of high achievement to some degree:

☐ The tiredness that comes from working an unsustainable schedule
☐ The envy you feel when a friend gets promoted
☐ The anxiety when a family celebration interferes with your work schedule
☐ The despair you feel when you miss a job opportunity
☐ The anger you feel when you make an innocent mistake

- ☐ The frustration when you have to work in a group and can't control every outcome
- ☐ The isolation, the loneliness, the fear of failing
- ☐ That never-ending feeling of complete exhaustion

There is research suggesting the eldest child in a family is more likely to be a high achieve.[1] Statistically, the eldest is more likely to be the most ambitious and well-qualified of all your family. But it's not just your birth order that can make you a pathological perfectionist—someone who feels obsessively driven to continually meet exceptional standards, no matter what toll it takes. Early experiences—especially if they're traumatic—can also be a factor in an overachieving personality, resulting in a strong desire to accomplish something important and gain gratification from success or external accolades.

My mum says that even as a toddler I lived at an accelerated pace, always busy and always striving. When I was ten, my class would be tested on their times tables every Friday and my dad and I spent two hours every night practising. It's not that I had pushy parents—they only did what I asked of them. My very high standards were not limited to my education either. I was a champion gymnast as a child and have run seven marathons. And then there was my stringent diet. It turns out pathological perfectionism is a common trait among people with eating disorders.

For a long time, I saw socialising as nothing more than a waste of time and money. In my first year at university I tried to embrace the drinking culture, but by the second year I couldn't keep up the pretence of caring. While my housemates were enjoying themselves I'd be slaving over my coursework. An ex-boyfriend told me, 'Amy, you're so driven but sometimes I don't think you're having fun along the way.' And he was right.

When I wrote that Daily Mail article I was 28 and working as the editor of a fashion magazine. On paper I had it all—an amazing job and all the stylish perks that came with it. But I never felt satisfied and any sense of pride only lasted for a second. Within a week of every promotion I'd be looking for the next achievement, the next status symbol and acknowledgement that I actually meant something. I was beginning to see how one-dimensional—not to mention joyless—a life fuelled by ambition can be.

I was also utterly exhausted. It came to a head one evening after my staff went home. I sat on the floor in my office and stared at the same spot on the wall—for three hours. I couldn't even allow myself to cry, because that would have been weak in my eyes. I was so driven that I had driven the life right out of my body. One of the definitions of perfect is 'absolute and complete' but I have never felt so empty.

☐ DO YOU HAVE AMBITION FATIGUE?

In recent years, researchers have begun to examine the dark side of ambition. A 2014 study found that perfectionism (defined as the setting of unattainable goals that are never enough) leads to an increased risk of pathological worry and anxiety disorders.[1] Separate research has linked extreme perfectionism to higher risks of addictions, irritable bowel syndrome and coronary disease. A new study from the

University of Kent found that 'sexual perfectionism' is also crushing women's libidos, as they struggle to look perfect and to perform perfectly in the bedroom.[1]

It's not only adults that are affected. In 2016, I wrote an investigation for Collective Hub about the alarming rate of teenage suicides in Silicon Valley. The principal of a high school in Palo Alto revealed that, in 2015 alone, 42 students had been hospitalised or treated for 'significant suicide ideation' and that 212 students had been identified as high-risk or at-risk.

Many of those troubled students blamed the pressure of trying to meet unattainable expectations. On the website Quora, one student from Palo Alto wrote: 'Going to school here is extremely hard and stressful. The standard is very high. It makes you feel worthless.' The students I spoke to talked about feeling crushed by their schoolwork and extracurricular activities in a school where it's not unusual for teenagers to already be running their own company or accepted into university at the age of fourteen.

On online forums, I found teenagers talking about the exhaustion they felt from trying to 'do it all' and excel in both their education and hobbies. A boy of seventeen nearly drowned in the swimming pool at Palo Alto Country Club, when he pushed himself too far practising underwater distance training. This is an extreme and heartbreaking consequence but, in a different context, can you relate to the pressure he experienced?

Have you ever felt like you're drowning in work, barely treading water?

Has your schedule—your expectations—ever left you gasping for air?

Constant striving can be both physically and mentally dangerous. Shortly after the report about teenage suicide, I wrote an article about a condition called 'brownout' and how it is becoming increasingly common among go-getters. The sibling of burnout, it is being used by psychologists, business coaches and academics to describe the stage before full burnout.

Symptoms include disengagement, discontentment and a general feeling of lethargy. In a study published in the Harvard Business Review, one participant summed it up by saying: 'Sometimes . . . I find myself actually hoping I'll have a heart attack. At least it would be an honourable way out'.' It might sound crazy but it's the result of pushing yourself to achieve more, constantly. I have a friend who regularly has panic attacks on the train station on the way to work, because she's cracking under the pressure.

When I was an editor I would definitely have fallen into the brownout category, one deadline away from full-blown burnout. At the weekend I would regularly wake up and cry, because I knew I had two options: to spend my weekend working or allow myself to rest then have to grapple with the guilt and anxiety that I felt whenever I took any downtime.

I am a big believer that, if you need to make changes in your life, the universe will give you a small nudge and then a big nudge—and then the message will be delivered in a way that you cannot ignore any longer. For some people it's a health scare (my friend who suffered from panic attacks was in a freak accident which left her housebound for months). In my case, I was made redundant when the magazine where I worked closed overnight.

The week the news broke was terrible for my staff, who were incredibly talented and dedicated. Although I felt sad for my team, I didn't feel any sadness for myself. In fact, I felt an incredible sense of relief. After a decade of striving to succeed, impress and progress I had been given an opportunity to break a vicious cycle. When I powered off my computer in that office for the last time, I decided it was time to flick a switch on my life.

☐ CHECKING INTO PERFECTIONIST REHAB

A couple of months after I was made redundant, the universe sent me another message. Despite vowing that I'd take a break to recuperate after the magazine closed, I had thrown myself ferociously into the freelance world— unsurprisingly. I was working longer hours than ever, as I feverishly pitched stories to multiple editors at multiple magazines in multiple countries. Perhaps I would have continued on that destructive career path, but help came from an unexpected source.

Late one night as I was scrolling through Facebook, I saw that a friend had commented on a post written by an American life coach, offering a self-help program called Perfectionist Rehab. I can't remember exactly what the post said, but it resonated so deeply with me I contacted Elli (the life coach) immediately, asking if I could do the program remotely.

I learnt that Elli's clients are successful, goal-orientated people, who exhaust themselves with a constant need to take their careers, relationships or exercise routines one step further. Around the same time I was made redundant, my relationship ended (out of respect for my ex-partner I won't go into details). Needless to say, it was a time of intense change, transition and growth for me.

Over the next six months I 'met' with Elli weekly—she sat in her office in Charleston while I Skyped from my sofa in Sydney. There were actually three people in our therapy sessions: me, Elli and my inner critic, Johanna—a short, dark-haired woman with tortoiseshell glasses who, for some reason, screamed in an American accent. I was sceptical when Elli told me to create a character for the voice in my head who was constantly saying I wasn't worthy. But I discovered that once I gave my inner critic a personality, she was far easier to reason with—or ignore completely.

'You have to try harder,' Johanna yelled. 'If you don't help yourself, then no-one else will.'

'I hear you Johanna,' I replied calmly. 'I know you're trying to change me. But what if I'm already good enough?'

There's also the emotional toll it can take, both on the sufferer and their loved ones. Constantly chasing dreams can be exhausting, and it's hard to maintain close relationships when you're always comparing yourself and competing with others. It's also an affliction more likely to affect women, as shown by studies that found the majority of women only apply for a promotion when they meet 100 percent of the qualifications, compared to men, who often apply when they meet just 60 percent. So, is perfectionism really an illness that needs to be cured?

'To a perfectionist, every action is black and white, good or bad,' said Elli. 'But learning to explore the grey area is part of the journey.' As part of my rehab homework, she instructed me to set my alarm an hour later than usual. She also suggested that, after I woke up, I wait for at least 45 minutes before checking my emails. A lot of perfectionists cram the first hour of the day with activities because they never wake up feeling good enough, so need to achieve something as soon as possible, to feel validated.

During the daytime, I was advised to follow the 60-60-30 method of productivity created by business coach Eben Pagan. You work intensively for one hour, then have a ten-minute break, followed by another hour of work. The final thirty minutes of the cycle should be spent doing something pleasurable, whether it's reading a book, calling a friend or just lying on your back deep breathing. As for evenings, rather than hitting the gym, I was instructed to do a very gentle yin yoga class at home—with a glass of wine before-hand to help me relax.

This might all sound blissful to B-type personalities but, for an A-type like me, it was incredibly tough to stick to. I missed the feeling of utter exhaustion that I usually felt at the end of the day, which signalled in my mind that I'd been productive. In the morning, I couldn't validate myself by the number of emails in my inbox or the speed setting on my treadmill. I was worried that if I let my standards slip, even a little, I'd become a directionless drifter who never got out of her pyjamas!

However as time went on, I realised the world didn't end if I had to push back a deadline, skipped a gym session or forgot to proofread an email and accidentally sent a kiss to my most important client (that did happen!). I became more compassionate to myself and also the people around me. I could feel genuinely happy when a friend got a promotion, without immediately searching job boards for my next step up the ladder.

Your perfectionist mentality may not warrant rehab (if you do, Elli's details are listed at the back of this book) but it's still worth keeping a close eye on. I've learnt that when I'm feeling stressed or enter a challenging time in my life, my inner perfectionist tends to emerge along with the unhealthy behaviour she encourages. I've learnt to recognise the signs: when I view my mornings as a tick-list, when I see exercise as a chore, when I stop chatting to strangers because I'm too busy.

By the time I checked out of perfectionist rehab I was less motivated, less ambitious and lazier than ever—and that made me a perfect student. One of the greatest achievements of my life has been not having to be the greatest at everything anymore.

☐ COPING WITH A CAREER CRISIS

Six months after I lost my magazine job, I interviewed the Australian entrepreneur, Nikki Durkin. The founder of the fashion website 99dresses had just published a blog post titled: My start-up failed and this is what it feels like . . . In 2014, after being hailed as a star in the start-up world, she walked away from the business she'd started as a nineteen-year-old, following financial difficulties. The closure of the company also meant she'd lost her American visa, so she had ten days to leave the country.

'Over 90 percent of tech start-ups fail, but I never thought my baby would be one of them,' wrote Nikki. 'We had users and traction, then we fell off a cliff. My four-year emotional rollercoaster just came to a head.' Within three days, the blog post had gone viral with over 250,000 views and Nikki had been hailed as a trailblazer for failure.

'I think your impulse is to rebound onto something else,' Nikki said. 'But I feel like I've just come out of a long-term relationship and I need to be "single" for a while. When I get to the point where I can think of an idea without feeling exhausted, I'll know that it's time to move forward.'

As well as over a hundred job offers, Nikki was sent care packages, restaurant vouchers and even given a free holiday to Nevada to help her rest and recover. Her flight home from LA to Sydney was paid for by a good Samaritan—the owner of a technology start-up in Australia, who heard that she couldn't afford her airfare.

Nikki's disappointment made her vulnerable, her failure made her approachable, and she was gracious enough to take help when it was offered. Three years later, Nikki is the founder of CodeMakers—an online program that aims to empower children by teaching them to code. She taught herself to meditate and takes time out every morning to sit quietly with a cup of coffee and count her blessings. She says the experience taught her to get better at picking herself up after failure and to work with people who complement her skill set, rather than trying to go it alone.

- How do you deal with a disappointment in your career?
- Are you still scarred by a rejection in your past?
- Has one boss' comments defined your career path?

This is a topic that has always interested me. I graduated from university shortly before the global financial crisis, so I don't know the meaning of a stable job market. I've only ever worked in a world where you're only as good as your last pay cheque, where redundancies are common and there's no guarantee of a renewed contract.

Although my résumé is impressive, it doesn't show the disappointments that pepper my career history—the book that wasn't published; the job interview I thought I'd nailed; the time the BBC bought the television rights to my first book, then cancelled production due to lack of funding (I still have the script in my filing cabinet along with a list of actresses I wanted to play me which I emailed over to the producer).

I have probably missed 70 percent of the career goals that I've set my mind to. The difference is I shoot for ten times more than the average person and I've learnt—with a lot of practise—not to cling to the failures too tightly. In a world where entire industries can crumble in a matter of months, even the most confident and capable professionals need to be prepared for their jobs to vanish. But it doesn't have to break you.

☐ REDUNDANCY IS THE NEW PROMOTION

This is the title of an article I wrote for Harper's BAZAAR magazine in Australia, about six months after my magazine folded. At that time, a lot of people were losing their jobs but, rather than holding them back, it was pushing them forward. I was living in Bondi Beach and in the middle of the workday, you could find groups of 'redundancees' sitting in cafes, excitedly brainstorming their next project and celebrating their new-found freedom.

'It's like a secret club,' said my friend Marisa, who had been made redundant from a not-for-profit that had had a funding cut. 'The morning after I lost my job, I remember meeting a friend for coffee. I thought she would feel sorry for me, but instead she was excited. She told me to look at it as a stepping stone to better things.' Marisa's redundancy gave her the space to train as a yoga teacher while working as a freelance consultant, and motivated her to move back to America to be close to her family.

- ○ What would you do if you lost your job tomorrow?
- ○ How would you celebrate your first day as a free man (or woman)?
- ○ How could you use that time and space to make yourself happier?
- ○ Who are you without your job title?

Every week, it seems like there is a headline about job cuts across a big corporation or industry. Yet rather than carrying a stigma, redundancy actually comes with bragging rights, as it proves that you're a survivor and can bounce back from disappointment. The secret, according to redundancees I've interviewed, is to not take the rejection personally. 'In this challenging economy, it's all about the bottom line,' said Marisa. 'On a logical level, I can see how restructuring the organisation and removing my role made smart business sense.'

In fact, you could argue that you're far more likely to be made redundant if you're in a position of power and value, because removing a senior salary from a company's outgoings will have a far greater effect than axing a junior role.

Of course, we can't gloss over the downsides of dismissal—most obviously, money worries sparked by the loss of a regular salary. Yet a job loss can actually make you more financially comfortable in the long run. A 2012 survey found that four out of ten workers made redundant from a corporate restructure ended up in another role which paid more. On top of this, a quarter of those surveyed got a more senior position after they lost their job[1].

And then there's the redundancy package! In a time where annual bonuses are a distant memory, and many companies have frozen pay rises, it's rare to be handed a lump sum—let alone one that comes with a tax break. People are using their payouts to fund round-the-world trips, housing deposits, maternity leave and even IVF treatment.

One of my former employees used her lump sum to move to LA—chasing a new career and an ex-boyfriend who had emigrated there. 'I don't feel any shame,' she said. 'In fact, when I'm meeting editors I often say that it's a rite of passage that everyone in publishing is probably going to go through at least once in their career. In an odd way, it shows you have experience and resilience. I've bonded with editors over their own job loss stories.' She is now not only a successful freelance writer, she is also expecting her first child with the lover she almost lost.

In any career, anything could happen tomorrow. You could lose your job or you could be offered a new one. You could be promoted or someone else could be promoted above you. Ever since my first husband died, whenever I've gone through a 'success drought' and nothing feels like it's going my way, I repeat the same mantra: Any phone call, any email, any meeting could be the one that changes your life forever. Life is one big surprise party. You can either jump at the party poppers or dance under the confetti.

☐ HOW TO BE HAPPY FOR OTHER PEOPLE'S ACHIEVEMENTS . . . WITHOUT FAKING IT.

◌ **Turn jealousy into empathy**
We've all experienced jealousy to some degree. Whether you're the office, in the gym or at a school reunion, we can't help comparing ourselves to others and seeing what we lack. Instead of envying a stranger from a distance, why not strike up a conversation? Ask them, for example, about their fitness routine, how long they've been practising, or what their tips are for advancing. It's far harder to be envious when you know the effort it took someone to reach that level.

◌ **Pick your role models wisely**
My sister is a competitive cyclist and former champion iron-woman. My mother, despite being incredibly fit for her age, is not a professional athlete. Yet she still compares herself to my sister whenever they work out together. Role models can be inspirational, but they also need to be relatable. Don't compare your career to that of an industry professional who

has been on the ladder since you were in nappies. If you start a new hobby, don't feel demoralised because someone who took it up years ago is ahead of you. That doesn't mean you can't be inspired by people more accomplished than you are, but use them as motivation rather than let them destroy your morale.

○ Celebrate your differences

I have a mantra that I repeat whenever I'm surfing with my husband, who first stepped onto a board when he was a toddler. As I'm battling the shallow whitewash and he's making barrels look easy, I repeat to myself: This is him and I am me. It might sound simple, but it reminds me to be proud of both of our achievements for different reasons. As a city girl from London, I'm proud that I took up a hobby in my thirties. I'm also proud that, for my partner, a lifetime of practice has paid off.

○ Think about your face

English author Thomas Browne once wrote: Let age, not envy, draw wrinkles on your cheeks. The truth is that envy is not a good look on anyone and it does reflect in our features, even if you don't realise it. I once caught a glimpse of myself in a gym mirror, glaring at a woman who could lift more weights than I could and it was not flattering! Next time you envy someone, force yourself to smile at them. You might even find yourself meaning it—and make a friend.

○ Don't be your best

Trying to be perfect at something can quickly make it unenjoyable, so purposefully force yourself to underperform and see what happens. When I'm in a yoga class and the teacher instructs everyone to do a handstand, I sometimes don't—even though I can—just to test my ego. Instead I join the novices with their legs up the wall. It's a good reminder that the world keeps spinning, whether or not you're on top of it.

NINE

Have I Said Too Little? Shyness and Oversharing

I once overheard a boyfriend talking about me to one of his friends. 'Amy either talks a lot or she doesn't say anything at all,' he said. 'She's either the loudest voice in the crowd or she disappears completely.' The friend he was talking to was my gym instructor. He was complaining about how I'd sometimes chat too loudly and excitedly at the start of group fitness class and he'd have to tell me to be quiet. On other occasions, I'd slink in silently, avoid eye contact and leave early, so I didn't have to engage in conversation.

At different periods of my life I have been described as shy, quiet, reclusive, loud, noisy, and an attention seeker. It might sound like a contradiction—and it is—but I have swung between oversharing and crippling shyness. I haven't always picked my audience wisely either. I have spilled all to strangers and then shut off my loved ones. I've clung to the wrong crowd but refused to bond with my colleagues.

I've walked down the street 'chatting' on a fake phone call to avoid human interaction. I've pretended to be sick, injured, stuck in the office and trapped in traffic to avoid a social occasion. On the flip side, I've bared my soul to 'friendly' drug dealers and declared my undying loyalty to a 'new best friend' whose surname I didn't even know (she later stole my credit card and spent $500 of my savings on cigarettes).

You would think that as a writer and storyteller I would be an expert in communication, but I'm far from it. I've veered between shyness and brashness. My inner introvert has left me lonely and my inner extrovert has left me vulnerable. It has taken me until the age of 33 to find some kind of balance between the two sides of my personality—to feel safe sharing myself with the people who love me and to stop craving attention from the waifs and strays I've met in dark alleys.

We are living in an age where we have hundreds of people in our virtual social circle and spend our days sending our thoughts into the wide world. Yet it feels like an increasing number of people are struggling to talk to each other on a genuine and authentic level. We are virtually connected, but increasingly lonely. We have hundreds of followers, but nobody we feel safe to confide in. We are also prone to exaggeration, filtering our lives so they catch other people's attention. Is what you say or type always 100 percent true? If not, why not?

- ◯ Who am I?
- ◯ Who am I pretending to be?
- ◯ And why do I need to pretend?

There's also the matter of discussing our failures and disappointments. We live in an age where everybody has a 'brand'—but how does a past tragedy, misfortune or difficult patch fit into that public image? If there's a rough patch in your past, should you share it and to who, how and when? On social media, we share our lunches, workouts and the inside of our bathrooms. But when is the right time to talk about trauma, tragedy and the smaller life events that have shaped us and changed us?

☐ OWNING YOUR STORY

In 2015, I interviewed Maggie Cino, senior producer of a storytelling event called The Moth. You may have heard of it. The Moth is an open mic night held across the world, where people are encouraged to tell true stories about experiences that have shaped them. You can also listen to the stories via their website and app. There's now even a telephone hotline which you can phone to record your own short story.

'Our goal is to help people find that memory,' said Maggie. 'The memory that is so true and so heartfelt, that it really burns them to speak. We want to create a place where it feels scary but also safe to share it.' It could be an unusual mission (a woman attempting to cross the Arctic); a testing situation (a college student spending a night in prison) or a personal revelation (why a guy left his fiancée at the altar).

The Moth even runs corporate programs with storytelling workshops, to help employees better communicate with each other. 'It's not possible to be anonymous anymore,' said Maggie. 'Your boss can search for you online and, if you made a terrible mistake when you were fourteen, someone will find out about it in five minutes. What's really powerful is owning who you are, being able to make decisions and choosing how, when and why you share personal information.'

- Is there a section of your life you feel the need to hide?
- Is there a version of yourself you don't talk about?
- Is there a secret in your past that you dread coming out?
- Why is this? What are you scared of?

My career has been spent encouraging people to tell their stories in an empowering way. I haven't always got it right. In my early twenties when I was a junior reporter, I had instances when I exaggerated people's stories to please editors, put words into people mouths that didn't belong and failed to do their stories justice (it's not something I'm proud of). I know I genuinely hurt some people I interviewed because I didn't 'polished' their sentences to make it more headline-worthy. Today I am meticulous about checking every sentence is an accurate reflection.

I've learnt that how people tell their own stories is an intimate experience and something as small as a replaced word or misplaced question mark can change the entire feeling of a story—and how that person feels about themselves.

These days, thanks to the internet, there are more ways than ever to tell your story, which is both a good and a bad thing. I once interviewed a 28-year-old woman who told her parents she had HIV by text message. I wrote about the rise of #divorceselfies—women who take photos of themselves holding their divorce papers outside their divorce hearing.

I also interviewed Penelope Trunk, the businesswoman who made headlines when she live-tweeted her miscarriage, while sitting in her office boardroom. When the tweet went viral, she faced backlash for sharing her experience on such a public forum. But she defended her decision: 'My tweet was a public service announcement' she said, revealing that she had lost another baby four years earlier. 'When I had my first miscarriage I was inconsolable. I didn't get out of bed for weeks. The worst aspect of it was that I didn't know how to tell people and nobody knew what to say to me.'

Although all of these women chose to share their stories in different ways—and you may or may not agree with their choice of medium—none of them regretted their decision to be open. This doesn't mean you have to walk around with a sign on your chest that lists your past failures and disappointments. But don't burn a chapter from the book of your life or your story won't make sense—to you or anyone else.

☐ FINDING YOUR VOICE

When I started dating again after my first husband died, I was adamant I didn't want to be thought of as a widow. So I hid my past from everyone (which is surprisingly easy to do in an anonymous city like London). I thought it would be liberating to wipe my past clean, but actually it was exhausting. The walls of my bedroom were covered with tape marks from where I'd stuck up photos from my wedding day, then ripped them down whenever I had a visitor. I felt like I was constantly lying (because I was), scared that my secret would be uncovered by my colleagues, by new friends and by the men I bought home from nightclubs.

Three years after my husband died I 'came out' in spectacular fashion. My first book Wife, Interrupted was published in bookshops around the country and then the world. It may seem strange that, although I wasn't comfortable talking about my past to anyone, I wrote a tell-all memoir about my experience of widowhood. Wife, Interrupted was the result of three years of writing, silently, in my bedroom. It was the only way I'd found to express myself authentically.

Unveiling the real 'me' wasn't easy. When the book was published I faced a lot of criticism, mainly from strangers, many of whom hadn't read past the book's description. I was called insensitive, disrespectful and heartless, for admitting that I grieved in an unorthodox way—by having sex with strangers. I was dubbed the 'scarlet widow' by a newspaper and told that I was dishonouring my husband's memory, by talking about such a sensitive subject.

My life would have been easier if I hadn't shared my experience so openly. Perhaps my late husband's family would still talk to me now and a Google search of my name would be far less divisive. However, I don't regret telling my story, because at that time it was my truth— even though my 'character' back then is very different to the person I am now.

You could say that book affected my personal 'brand.' I'm sure it deterred some men who virtually stalked me before our dates. But I I had also made a promise to my husband that, if I ever wrote about our story, I would do it

100 percent honestly and write about what really happened, rather than what I thought people might like to hear. In fact, I turned down a book deal six months after Eoghan died, because that particular publisher wanted me to make my story 'a little more conventional.'

On my journalling retreats I always tell people to write exactly as they talk, and that's what I did with my book. I didn't overthink, overedit or overcorrect myself. I also didn't oversell the book once it was published. I sent it out into the world and trusted that it would find its way into the hands of people who needed it—and, from the thank you letters I received, it worked..

I still have an email that I was sent from an 84-year-old grandmother, after an extract from my book appeared in a newspaper. She had lost her husband when she was 23, during World War Two. In the email she admitted that, like me, she had become promiscuous after his death. 'After my husband was killed I slept with many men,' she wrote. 'I've been carrying that secret for over sixty years. It's only after reading your book that I can let that guilt go.'

When you find a way to tell your story authentically it doesn't just help you, but also people around you. When you give a little bit of yourself, it gives them permission to give a little bit of themselves back to you.

☐ SPEAK WHEN YOU HAVE SOMETHING BETTER TO SAY THAN SILENCE

These days I choose my confidants carefully. I trust my gut feeling, when it comes to how much I reveal about myself. When I do talk about my past, I try to constantly check in with myself: am I exaggerating, dramatising or changing my story to suit the person who is listening? I try to use fewer words but the right words. I have learnt to share relevant details of my life, without feeling the need to tell my entire life story. If I don't share my story, it's because I don't think it will benefit the person that I'm speaking to.

I have work colleagues that I've known for years who know nothing about my past—unless they Google me—because we're not really on the same mindset. By contrast, I can meet a stranger in a cafe, instantly click, and share my life story by the bottom of a cup of coffee. It might sound like a contradiction but I think this combination is a good thing. It allows my introvert to feel safe and my extrovert to feel acknowledged.

My dad has taught me the most about how to own your story, without letting it own you. Now that he's in remission he doesn't often talk about his cancer; but when he does it's with a purpose, usually to help someone else in a similar situation. Whenever he talks about being paralysed, he discusses it in the third person ('the legs wouldn't work' rather than 'my legs wouldn't work'). I think that allows him to share his worst memories while keeping them at a distance, so he can feel in control of them.

I'm not saying you should greet every new person with your name, age, number of sexual partners and a timeline of your past disasters. However, to form lasting relationships, platonic or otherwise, I think it's important to be open to sharing your story, when the time feels right. Perhaps this means you'll write your own book one day, phone up The

Moth hotline, or sit on a park bench with a stranger and talk about the terrible day you've just experienced. A confession should be an acknowledgement that the person you're confiding in matters.

☐ SEVEN EXPRESSIONS TO ERASE FROM YOUR VOCABULARY

1. I'm devastated
Are you really? A city is devastated by an earthquake. The world may be devastated by global warming. Unless your crisis is on the same scale, use a different adjective and give yourself hope for recovery.

2. I'll never forgive myself if . . .
You're already condemning yourself to a lifetime of guilt before an event has even happened. I try to avoid using 'never' when it comes to my feelings ('I'll never be happy again'), because nothing in life is conclusive.

3. I'm dreading it
You might be, but saying it aloud only reinforces it. If you do have concerns about an upcoming event or situation, be specific when you talk about your worries ('I feel nervous about seeing this person because . . .'). Then you might get closer to finding a solution.

4. I feel fat/ugly
I made a conscious decision when I started dating my husband that I'd never say this sentence in front of him, even when I felt it. When I muted my inner critic, it made a huge change to my body image.

5. How could you do this to me?
Okay, you may feel hurt by a situation, but everything you feel is your own responsibility. It's not what is said or done to you that makes you feel a certain way. It's what you do with what is said or done.

6. I can't believe it
Acceptance is the first step to healing. Even if a situation feel surreal, dig your heels into your new reality and feel its solidity. The sooner you accept it, the sooner you can adapt to it.

7. Why me?
Why not you?

☐ DO YOU NEED AN EXPERT OPINION?

I have an 'emotional entourage'. That's what I call the team of mentors, teachers and healers I rely on for support and guidance. Spread across the world, in different countries and cities, I credit them with helping me to find emotional contentment. In Sydney, I regularly see a psychotherapist for face-to-face sessions; I Skype with a life coach in South Carolina; I have long-distance healing from a spiritual healer in London; and I sporadically visit a hypnotherapist, a reiki practitioner and a meditation tutor. I've also seen a break-up coach and a divorce mentor, who helped me to compassionately exit my marriage.

It might sound excessive, having six experts on speed dial. But I've never regretted the time or money spent on these multiple touchpoints. Their professional skills don't overlap—my psychotherapist specialises in post-traumatic stress disorder, my hypnotherapist is an expert in 'mummy issues' and my spiritual healer teaches me to trust my gut instinct. When their powers are combined, they can banish any emotional demon. They're like The Avengers of mental health and they make me feel invincible.

Why am I telling you this? Because I'll take any opportunity to talk about them, not because it helps me but because I hope it helps other people. Sadly, there still seems to be a stigma around the subject of therapy, although it is gradually improving. It's amazing how many of my friends (or friends of friends) have approached me in confidence to ask if I can recommend a therapist for them. They always seem embarrassed or email me in secret ('Please don't tell anyone I asked you'). They feel shame or think it shows weakness, but in fact it's quite the opposite.

In every other area of our lives we don't think it's odd to enlist an expert. If I have a sore throat I see a doctor, when I need to get fit I see a trainer, and I would never let my best friend cut my hair when I can afford a stylist. So why, when it comes to mental wellbeing, are people so reluctant to admit they need professional assistance? Most of us don't wake up enlightened, balanced and empowered—even that 'perfect' person you think has the answer to everything. At times we all need an outsider's opinion and a fresh pair of eyes to see the demons on our periphery.

I'm not saying therapy is right for everyone, but be open to signs that you should explore it. It's also important that you find a healer who is right for you. When I was sixteen, I visited my first therapist when I was admitted to an eating disorder clinic. I didn't get on with her at all—which is more of a criticism of my mindset than of her skills—and it put me off seeing a therapist for years. I didn't realise that, like yoga teachers and masseuses, certain people will respond to different techniques and approaches.

The best thing you can do is be open to every healing opportunity. I discovered my hypnotherapist after I was sent to review a health retreat by a magazine I worked for. I really didn't want to go—it was a busy time of year in magazine world—and I certainly didn't want to emotionally purge while I was there. But before I knew it, I was lying on my back on the hypnotherapist's couch, sobbing my heart out, because I'd been 'visited' by my seven-year-old self who just wanted to be loved (more on that later!).

If you know that one of your friends is undertaking some form of therapy, healing or guidance, then ask them about it. I love passing on the details of my entourage to anyone who I feel could benefit from their insight. I've listed their details at the back of this book for anyone who is interested. I encourage you to use them as a starting point for embarking on your own journey.

In the short term, it might feel like therapy is doing more harm than good, especially when you emerge from a session in tears after handing over your credit card. But if you divide that emotional and financial expenditure over a lifetime, it's nothing. When you're celebrating your seventieth birthday will you regret the investment? I doubt it!

These days I don't talk to any of my emotional entourage regularly. But I do know they're there if I need a top-up.

Asking for help doesn't mean you're weak and it doesn't mean you'll become dependent on their guidance forever. There is a certain comfort in knowing you have a team of professionals on call in case of emergency. Sometimes we can all benefit from a second—or sixth—opinion.

TEN

Feeling 'Fleeful'?
The Search for a Safe Place

Whenever a horrific tragedy happens in the public eye—a natural disaster, a brutal murder or a plane crash—my editors ask me to find someone who has been through something similar. In 2011, when 92 people were killed by a lone gunman in Norway, I reached out to Marjorie Lindholm, one of the survivors of the Columbine shootings. She was just a teenager when, on 20th April 1999, she was caught up in one of America's worst-ever school shootings, when two pupils went on a killing spree murdering twelve classmates and one teacher before taking their own lives.

'At the moment, the survivors of Norway will be in shock,' said Marjorie. 'But that will only protect them for so long. Next will come the flashbacks, the night terrors and the panic attacks, every time a police siren goes off.' She had hidden in a classroom, while the shooters held people hostage in the gym hall, and said the location had a lasting effect on her. 'It's moulded the adult I've become, from where I live, to my relationships and where I work,' she said. 'I had to study my degree online, because I cannot sit in a classroom. I was a straight-A student before that day and had never seen violence firsthand. When you nearly lose your life in a place which is supposedly safe, it makes you question everything.'

I can't imagine how it would feel to survive such an atrocity. But in a different way, I think we can all relate to the idea that certain spaces should be 'safe'—and thus our shock if something unpleasant happens there. We are brought up to believe that our homes should be happy, our school days are the best days of our lives and university is a place where people thrive. But that's not always true.

When you believe a space should be safe it makes it even harder if, for whatever reason, we find ourselves feeling fearful, lonely or heartbroken there. The same applies to people. What happens when the people who are supposed to make us feel happy, safe and protected can no longer meet these obligations . . . or don't want to?

- ○ When you imagine yourself standing in your childhood home, how do you feel?
- ○ When you imagine standing in your old school hall, how do you feel?
- ○ In the bedroom of your first real boyfriend? In your parents living room?
- ○ What thoughts does your supposedly safe place evoke?
- ○ How do you feel at the thought of being there—or being forced to leave there?

My mother is the daughter of immigrants who moved to England from Ireland when they were in their twenties. When she was growing up, she was taught by her Catholic parents that inside their house was the only safe place and that the outside world—the bustling city of London—was a dangerous, risky place where anything could happen. It was better to stay put, to mix with 'your own kind' and never go too far. Because of this, she grew up with an over attachment to home, as a place that should always be on your side and shield you.

In theory, this is a positive lesson to teach a child—far better than thinking of home as a place filled with fear. But there is a downside. When my dad got cancer my mum's belief that home is a protective space was rocked. Home was no longer safe. Home was the place where my dad woke up unable to feel his legs. A place that had to be sterilised, ruthlessly, because one infection could kill him. One day, my mum came back from a jog to find my dad bleeding out on the couch from a blood clot. Later, home was where she heard the news that my husband had cancer and where she was standing when I called to say that it had spread to his brain.

Her childhood meant she was conditioned to see the outside world as a risky place, but now her home was unsafe too. If I convinced her to come out on a shopping trip, within half an hour of leaving the house she would become panicked and feel the need to go home and check on my father. But as she got closer to home she would become even more afraid, not knowing what she might find there.

☐ HOME IS WHERE THE HEARTBREAK IS

You might relate to this feeling, if you've ever felt challenged in your own personal space. If you had a difficult relationship with your parents as a teenager ('you're under our roof'); if you were bullied at school; or, as an adult, shared a home with a partner long after your relationship turned toxic. Suddenly, your happy home (possibly even your dream home) becomes a place of awkward silences, pursed lips and icy exchanges.

When I was seventeen, my home became a place where I had to avoid meals, tell lies and silently cry into a pillow after taking too many laxatives. When I was eighteen, my home became a place where I threw a wild party a few weeks before my dad was diagnosed with cancer—a reminder that I was a terrible daughter. When I was 21, my home was a place where my husband fell into a coma, where we fought because I'd caught him smoking, and where I'd hear him through the wall of the bathroom, vomiting up green fluid.

Unlike my mother who struggled to leave the house, these incidents had the opposite effect on me. I became a fleer. When my dad was ill, I fled from England to Australia. After my husband died, I fled from Ireland to England. In a decade, I moved house more than twenty times. I have a box of spare keys in the bottom of my wardrobe but have no idea which door they fit—or even what country that door is in.

Even when I stayed in one home for an extended period, I didn't emotionally unpack there. I hated spending money on furniture and would buy only the bare essentials. I wanted to know that if anything bad happened, I could cut ties in an instant and move without having to ask anyone to help me.

If I grew too attached to a place I'd go into self-sabotage mode—pick a fight with my housemate or kiss the boy she liked (not proud!), so that I'd be forced to move on and cut my losses. I thought I was the only person who did this until I moved to Australia and ended up at Bondi Beach, which I soon discovered is a mecca for fleers like me.

During my first week beside the pool, I met a girl whose boyfriend had died when he was BASE-jumping. At a coffee shop, I struck up a conversation with a woman writing a book about her violent ex-boyfriend who she'd left behind in England. In every yoga workshop I attended, you could be sure that someone with a foreign accent would have a personal story to tell—and it wouldn't be a fairytale.

As fleers we congregated together, telling each other that it was okay that we never phoned home and had no plans to visit. After I moved to Australia, I didn't go back to England for three years, always making excuses that I was too busy at work or didn't have the money. The truth is I was scared—I think a lot of us were—to remember where I had come from. I was also scared to build a new, permanent home in Australia—or anywhere—in case it came crashing down around me.

☐ THE GREAT ESCAPE

This is not a criticism of fleeing. My search for safety has taken me to some amazing places. If I'd stayed in Ireland, I don't think I could have processed my grief as well as I did.

If I'd stayed in England when my dad was sick, then I truly believe he would have outlived me. I know fleers whose flight path has led to incredible achievements. An entrepreneur I know left Ireland after an abusive relationships to work for a children's charity in Kenya. Another friend moved to South Africa and launched a start-up, offering sex education to young girls.

I'm grateful that my own escape route brought me to Australia and the life I've now created. But what about when you want to stop starting over?

I had lived this way for so long that I didn't really know anything different. But I began to see the downside to my 'fleeful' lifestyle. I couldn't plan ahead more than six months, because I didn't trust where my life would be. I lived in a transient area among transient people, so I didn't form lasting, intimate relationships. I always had a sense that I couldn't live this way forever and needed to be open to signs that it was time to stop running. And then one came.

On my first date with my current husband, he invited me to his house for a takeaway. At the time I was homeless, having deciding to move out of my old apartment after a disagreement with my flatmate. I was storing all of my belongings in a damp car park under my friend's apartment block and sleeping on her pull-out sofa. I remember telling him on one of our early dates, 'I love living like this. It's so incredibly liberating.'

But my nomadic existence would soon be over.

When I walked into his apartment, I remember having this overwhelming feeling: I am going to live here. I am going to be incredibly happy here. It was crazy, because we were only on date one and were really total strangers. But as we sat in his apartment making small talk and finding out about each other, I felt like the energy of the room was cushioning me. I was safe, I was whole and I was home. I didn't want to go anywhere ever again.

I still have a 'fleeful' instinct in me. Although I'm incredibly grateful to have a home, I will always feel slightly vulnerable here. Today, we live in a beautiful house by the ocean, in many ways the home of our dreams. But I sometimes get scared about what these walls will see, if we stay here for a lifetime: the struggles that might be ahead of us; the bad days, the cross words and the silent tears muffled by shower water. If we have one small disagreement within these four walls I'll think: 'This house is ruined. We'll always associate it with a bad memory.' I'll have mentally packed our bags and be scanning estate agents websites. But that's a side effect of my past that I'm learning to rationalise and not react to.

These days, I love going home to visit my parents in England, despite the fact that I can picture my dad in his wheelchair in the living room and my dead husband's coat still hangs in their downstairs closet. When I last went home, I asked my mum to show me old photographs from my childhood and we talked about happy times we shared as a family. It made me remember that, for all the tears that had been cried in that place, the walls had also vibrated with laughter on many more occasions.

I have the utmost respect for anyone who stays in a place where they have faced misfortune. I watched an incredible TED Talk about the elderly women who still live at the site of the world's worst nuclear accident ('Why stay in Chernobyl? Because it's home'). Perhaps our generation are too quick to cut cords and disassociate ourselves from a place that has stirred up negative emotions.

I wouldn't discourage anyone from leaving a place, if they believed it would help them to heal from a past situation. But I'd also encourage all serial fleers to examine what they are fleeing from, and whether they still need to. They might discover the danger they are escaping from doesn't exist anymore.

☐ HOW TO WIPE A PLACE CLEAN

○ Reclaim it

You have a choice to interact with a space in a positive or negative way. When I went back to England for the first time after moving to Australia, I stood in my old bedroom and silently repeated to myself, 'I take back this space. I choose to make it a positive place for me. I choose to be light, bright and happy here.' Today, I do this in my house whenever I feel negativity clogging the air, especially if I've had a challenging conversation in that space or any kind of professional confrontation. You can do it in your own home, your office, your parents' house or any space that makes your shoulders tighten. Always remember that a house is only a container for energy, either positive or negative, and that you have the power to change it.

○ Smudge it

I am a smudge stick addict. In Native American communities, herbs like sage and cedar are burned to heal and cleanse the mind, body and spirit. You can either make your own (there are YouTube videos showing you how) or buy a ready-made smudge stick from any hippyish store or eBay. Walk around each room, from corner to corner, with the smudge stick lit. I like to open a window and imagine the negative energy attaching to the smoke, then as the smoke dissipates, so does the negativity. I do the same with my Tibetan chimes: I walk around the house, sounding them in the corners of every room and letting the sound vibrate through any emotional fog in the air. It's also good to clean any objects you interact with regularly, like your computer or phone, especially after a difficult interaction.

○ Declutter it

Sometimes a good old-fashioned spring-clean can work wonders. This doesn't mean you have to clean your house from top to bottom; just pick one area that feels like it needs cleansing. Studies have shown that a decluttered space reduces stress levels, helps you to concentrate, boosts your mood and increases creativity. One study found that people who sleep in uncluttered bedrooms are less lightly to suffer from insomnia. Even the act of decluttering is soothing. Use it as an opportunity to meditate, as you mop the floors and swipe the fingerprints from your mirrors. In his book, The Miracle of Mindfulness, Buddhist monk Thich Nhat Hanh talks about mindful housework saying, 'The mustard greens I am planting are me. I plant with all my heart and mind. I clean this teapot with the kind of attention I would have were I giving the baby Buddha or Jesus a bath.'

⊃ **Personalise it**

When I interviewed Australian entrepreneur Lorna Jane Clarkson about her home, she told me she never hangs pictures up. She leaves them on the floor resting against a wall, because she loves to move them around so regularly. If you want your energy to flow through your house, make the interior decor flexible. I've realised that I can channel my transient energy into my decor. Move the furniture around, rearrange the paintings, hang free-flowing sarongs over the windows and place odd objects on the walls (we have a skateboard hanging up in our living room). When it comes to decorating, follow your senses. What colours make your relax? What textures make your feel nurtured? I just painted one wall of our baby's room moss green. It's not the most obvious choice for a little girl's nursery, but every time I see it I smell the essence of a forest.

⊃ **Create in it**

In my experience, creativity can light up any stagnant space. When we moved into our new house, my first project was to create my perfect writing space. I didn't have a specific image of what I'd like it to look like, but I did know what I wanted it to feel like—professional yet quirky, creative and colourful but practical. We eventually found the ideal standing desk, which is actually a kitchen bench from IKEA. It has enough space on it for my iPad, my pile of inspirational books and a small version of my altar (more on that later). I knew my home would feel more alive once I started writing in it. For you, being creative could mean baking, singing, dancing or inviting your friends around to be creative for you. I love it when my friends bring their children around—we lay a long roll of paper across the floor and hand out crayons. I can almost see their excitement light up the walls!

ELEVEN

Scared of the Dark? When Sleep Isn't Peaceful

When I was ten years old, I started having the same recurring nightmare at least once a month. In my dream I was in our living room, standing in front of my mirror with my dad. I was pulling at clumps of his hair which were coming out in my hand. I remember that in the dream I knew this meant something very, very bad, although at that point I had no experience of cancer. Seven years later, as I stood in front of a mirror with a father who'd just begun chemotherapy, I realised the recurring dream had come true. We had moved house since I was younger, so the room wasn't exactly the same; but my actions were identical—as was the unforgettable feeling.

In hindsight, this was not the only premonition (for want of a better word) that I had as a child. I would dream vividly, often telling my mum that my head was 'too full of thoughts' or 'my dreams are making me tired.' Sometimes I would see a scene, sometimes I'd just remember a feeling. Only later, would I link it to an event when it actually happened.

As an adult, these kind of dreams have continued. Last year, my best friend in Sydney had an accident at 2am. She was coming home from a night out, lost her keys and fell while trying to climb in her bathroom window. She laid for hours in the cold with a broken leg and ribs, before someone heard her calling out for help. At the time I was living in a different city, but that same night, over 200km away, I had a dream that I was standing in her apartment searching for her, feeling overwhelmed with panic. When I woke up, I felt shaken. Less than ten minutes later she called me from the hospital, just before she was taken into surgery.

For some people, dreams like this might seem terrifying. Other people might be sceptical and doubt whether humans have the ability to see the future in their dreams. But you've probably all experienced a night where reality infiltrates your dreams and affects what you see, do and feel in that state of consciousness: a person who keeps popping up in your dreams, even though you haven't seen them in years; a feeling of fear, loss, anxiety, love, joy or happiness that stays with you all day, even after you've woken up.

○ Have you ever slept on a question and woken up with the answer?

○ Have you ever gone to sleep feeling anxious and woken up feeling joyful?

○ Have you ever woken from a dream still feeling the touch of someone who was in it?

◌ Has a dream changed your view of a person or situation? Should you let it?

In my twenties, when I realised that some of my dreams had a tendency to come true, I felt a sense of fear at first. What if I saw something that I didn't want to? Is it really healthy to know what is coming, especially when you have no idea if a dream is a premonition or just a fantasy? Over time, I've learnt to appreciate these night-time narratives and to use them to my advantage, as either a guide or a warning.

When we sleep, our inhibitions step out of our way. It's probably the closest you come to thinking freely, so make the most of it.

☐ WHILE YOU WERE SLEEPING

I'm certainly not an expert when it comes to dream analysis. I do own a book on dream meanings, but I rarely open it. However, I do believe that being aware of your dreams and their meanings is useful, not only in helping you to create your ideal future but also for pinpointing traumas from your past that are holding you back.

Some dream meanings are more obvious than others. Years ago, when I was in a relationship that wasn't beneficial to either of us, I used to physically run in my dreams. I would lay horizontally in bed, with my legs whirring around like I was pedaling a bicycle. I stayed in that relationship for longer than I should have—we both did—despite my dream state telling me that we needed to move in different directions, quickly.

Some dreams are easier to read than others. I became teetotal in my early twenties, when I realised that, to find ease in my life, I needed to be sober. I also kept having a recurring dream that I'd accidentally drunk alcohol or taken drugs, and I was waiting for the effects to hit me. In the dream I felt a deep sense of dread and foreboding, because I knew that at any moment I'd feel a strange sensation and lose control of myself. I've been sober for nearly ten years and yet I still have the same dream sometimes, especially if my waking life is testing me.

I also believe the location of your dreams can be very telling. The majority of my nightmares are set in the house I lived in during my teenage years—a time when I was wrestling with my self-image, trapped in a toxic relationship and in conflict with my family.

A dream can draw attention to an event in your past that you still need to reconcile. As I've mentioned, my sister and I were both dangerously premature babies, with traumatic birth stories. Over thirty years later, my mum still has a recurring dream that she's cradling a tiny baby made of china, and she accidentally snaps her head off. In the dream she's overwhelmed with guilt, because she didn't look after the baby well enough.

My dad, who had a difficult relationship with a family member, never remembers his dreams—ever. He has a tendency to repress feelings and memories from his childhood. After the death of that family member, I dreamt that he came to see me and handed me a letter to give my father. When I opened it the letter read: I'm sorry.

Most of us, if we dig deep, have experienced dreams with a deeper meaning. When I was writing this chapter, I posted a request on Facebook. I asked whether anyone was happy to share a recurring dream which, in some way, had made them look twice at their lives. I thought that, if anything, one or two friends would message me privately. However, my post gradually turned into a buzzing message thread as people shared their dreams and the messages they'd uncovered within them.

One of my friends moved to another city after she kept dreaming about snakes (a symbol of transformation or change). An incredible entrepreneur I know, whose father died when she was young, ended an unhealthy relationship because of a dream in which she was running through a hospital, being chased by the man that she was dating. 'Every time I tried to run through a door, I realised it didn't have a lock on it,' she said. 'Finally, after a massive struggle, he attacked me and killed me . . . by kissing me!'

I also heard from a female friend who, unbeknown to me, had spent her twenties trapped in an abusive relationship. After she left her ex-partner, he stalked her for years. 'I used to have a recurring dream that someone was following me,' she said. 'Those dreams continued for years until one day, in my dream, I stopped running and turned around. I never had it again.' When the dream persisted, she began seeing a psychologist and underwent EMDR (Eye Movement Desensitisation and Reprocessing) treatment. 'I had some pretty crazy dreams after that, as I was processing a lot of old feelings and behaviours,' she said. 'But I feel like those dreams helped to complete the EMDR work I did, releasing old unhealthy thoughts I had.' She revealed that my husband and I were in one of those dreams and played a part in her healing.

Not every dream is significant. If you've binge watched a drama show, your dreams may be full of police cars and explosions. This doesn't mean you're going to end up in a hostage situation. I've learnt to recognise when I've had 'a dream that's more than a dream,' as I say to my husband next morning. When my dreams carry an important message, they feel crisper and clearer. It feels like a visitation rather than a vision.

During my pregnancy, I've been reading an amazing book called Dream Birth by Catherine Shainberg. It talks about the power of 'conscious dreaming.' Catherine invites people to ask a question before they go to sleep every night, then write it down in a notebook and offer an intention to accept what they must know. I decided to try it.

A few weeks after I found out I was pregnant, we packed up and moved to another city. It was a nine-hour drive from our home. My husband had been given the opportunity to work on an amazing job for three months (which turned into five), and I was excited about the move. But dramatically relocating at such a changeable time in my life had an unexpected side effect. For the first time in my life, I was suffering from crippling writer's block, uninspired and unmotivated to be creative. So before bed every night for a week, I wrote these words in my dream diary: Where is my creativity? And then I waited for an answer.

The first night I dreamt that I was at a house party full of people. I was trying to tell a story about something I did at work, but my husband kept talking over me. In the end I gave up and went to sit on my own in the bathroom. The second night I dreamt that I was standing outside a hut next to a river. A family approached and asked if I'd go to church with them. When I asked why they said, 'Because when people hear that you're spiritual, it seems okay for them to be.' On the third night I dreamt that we were living in a cottage in a forest. It was bright and light, with a huge bed covered in colourful fabrics and rainbow wall-hangings. We were living with lots of people—some we knew and some we didn't. I felt so happy and so loved. In my dream, I introduced a friend to my husband. 'You love him so much,' she said. 'It's true,' I replied. 'Every morning when I wake up, I wonder if it will all be gone—and then it's still there!'

I persisted with that dream query for a solid week. On the seventh—and final—night of asking the question, I dreamt I was at our baby's christening. I needed to find a paintbrush, although I didn't know why. So I went into an artist's studio which had huge murals on the walls. I picked up a paint roller and began adding to someone else's art. I felt a wave of contentment and happiness that, even after I woke up, stayed with me for the entire day.

At the end of the week I read back my dreams in sequence, and the message within their narratives became apparent. I was feeling overshadowed and slightly begrudging that we'd relocated for my husband's job, which meant that my work had taken second place. I needed to remember why I was a writer in the first place—to help and inspire people with my words and stories. Most significantly I was lonely, because we were living in a new city and I was missing human connection.

These dream meanings enabled me to make small, conscious changes. Every day, I made sure that I went to a cafe with a roaring fireplace, where the locals were friendly and I could enjoy wonderful, random conversations with strangers. I reached out to the editor of a website that I admired and asked if he wanted to work together. I could work alone but, at this point in my career, I wanted to 'add to someone else's painting.'

For me, the most important step is to learn to welcome your dreams—even the bad ones. Imagine if we could teach children to search for meaning in the monsters that hide under their beds? If we could make peace with the darker side of our minds, that often emerges only when we're in slumber. Over the years, I've learnt that my premonitions aren't a warning but a dress rehearsal. They're a chance for me to practise how I want to feel, react and cope when a traumatic event happens.

If you start to question where your life is going, if your plans have hit a friction point or you can't shake a certain feeling and if you can't find the answer by analysing your waking life, it could be time to throw the question to your dreamscape. Send your worries out into the night, then repeat the exercise over and over until you've found the answer. It's the best kind of therapy, because all you need to do is lie back and close your eyes,

When I was gathering stories for this chapter, a friend contacted me privately to tell me the most incredible story. When she was a teenager, her brother kept having the same recurring dream. He was standing in a field full of grass and a little girl that he didn't know approached him. She asked if she could have his legs. He liked the little girl, so he gave his legs to her as a gift. This dream continued for a year, until his waking life caught up with it. Unbeknown to anyone, her brother had a spinal tumour. One day it hemorrhaged and he was left permanently paralysed. He never had that recurring dream again, but says he always remembers one significant aspect of it—he had the choice whether or not to give the girl his legs and he wanted to. He knew that he would be okay without them.

Bedtime affirmations for a peaceful night's sleep

Before I go to sleep, even when (especially when!) I've had a tough day, I say one of these affirmations to ease myself into unconsciousness. You can either say one per night or, if they all resonate with you, weave them together into a prayer. Cut out and stick these by your bed tonight:

- ☐ I release my thoughts from today.
- ☐ I have earned my rest for today.
- ☐ I am excited for tomorrow.
- ☐ I am devoted to tomorrow.
- ☐ I flow into my dreams.
- ☐ I am in rhythm with the world.
- ☐ I let go of struggle.
- ☐ I choose peace.

TWELVE

Nature and Nurture: Stepping Outside Yourself

Towards the end of my second marriage, I flew back to England alone to visit my parents. Every time I go back to the UK I book an appointment with my spiritual healer, Yvonne, who I've been seeing for guidance since before I was widowed. When I walked into her house, the first thing she said was, 'There's another man coming into your life.' She told me that this man, who I didn't yet know, had an extremely masculine energy and spent a lot of time in nature. In a previous life he'd been a medicine man in South America and so, in this incarnation, he had a great interest in plants and their properties.

Over the years that I've been seeing Yvonne I've become very good at trusting her revelations, without obsessing about them. I know from experience that her predictions can take years to unfold. I did, however, go back to Australia and end my marriage immediately; not because she told me to, but because her words unleashed a truth that I had long been avoiding.

I packed up my life, moved out of the apartment my husband and I owned, and moved in with a friend who was looking for a flatmate. Justin, my new living partner, ran a not-for-profit organisation called Responsible Runners, dedicated to reducing rubbish on Australia's beaches. At the time he was organising a charity expedition across the Tarkine rainforest in Tasmania. The team planned to spend seven days running 140km across the wilderness—and they needed another member.

I had never done anything like that in my life. I hadn't been camping since I was a kid and I never ran on anything but tarmac. However, I didn't just agree to join the crew, I also volunteered to handle the publicity and sponsorship. I spent the next two months learning all there was to know about adventure gear, lightweight tents, hiking packs and the best gaiters to protect our legs from snakes in the undergrowth.

In December, three weeks before we set off for Tasmania, the entire expedition crew met for the first time at our apartment. There were nine people in the team including myself, and I had met seven of them before. The only thing I knew about the final team member was that he was an environmental scientist who had been training by running up and down sand dunes.

When our apartment door opened and our eighth mystery team member walked inside, I was sitting on the living room floor, so the first thing I noticed was his bottom half—hiking boots, muddy cargo pants and a chunky silver belt buckle. His first impression screamed adventure.

A week later we went on a team bonding trip, canyoning in the Blue Mountains west of Sydney. After I abseiled down a waterfall, he was waiting at the bottom lying on a rock that was warm from the sun. I was shivering and he told me to come and lie down next to him.

There is a photo of the two of us taken from the top of the waterfall by one of our teammates—it shows a girl and a boy lying so close together you can't see where one person ends and the other begins. I can't say I fell in love with him at the moment—it wasn't that obvious a realisation. I just knew that, whatever form our relationship took, I needed to be near him always.

We set off for the rainforest a few weeks later. For a former London girl, this was entirely out of my comfort zone. Yet somewhere among the trees, while I was covered in mud, sleeping in a tent and digging my own toilet, I discovered a part of myself that I didn't know I'd lost— and didn't know I'd missed until I found it!

Every night, we would sit in a hammock, eating dehydrated food out of plastic bowls, talking about our lives as the forest buzzed around us. He taught me about the plants and their properties, giving me leaves to eat as we hiked and telling me about their uses. He told me that he'd always dreamed of travelling across South America. Two years later he proposed to me in Peru, on a hike to the sacred city of Machu Picchu.

We stood among the trees,
One bag for you, one bag for me,
You didn't judge, you let me be,
Until I asked if you'd teach me.

We travelled light, our bags were packed,
I pressed my belly on your back,
I needed warmth, you said 'lie down'
We left one imprint in the ground.

You taught me how to cry,
Unleashed stars into the sky,
I float above you in the sea,
Won't break your heart, don't rebreak me.

In retrospect, this was not the first time I had found healing and meaning after immersing myself in nature. Although I spent my early twenties in the concrete jungle of London, when I think back to milestone moments in my life I've always gravitated towards nature for healing—swimming in the freezing Irish Sea with my husband, three days before he died; walking barefoot through the grass outside my dad's hospital; and praying to Pachamama (Mother Earth) for guidance, now that I'm a mother-to-be.

Since that trip to the rainforest, spending time in nature has become a crucial part of my healing process and a vital coping mechanism. When I'm happy, I hike. When I'm sad, I hike even further. When I feel ungrounded, I stand in the garden and visualise tree roots growing out of the soles of my feet, burying deep into the soil and earthing me, physically and emotionally.

There is amazing research confirming that a 'micro break' in nature of just ten minutes a day can dramatically reduce stress levels, anxiety and depression, as well as also boost productivity and creativity at work. One study of office workers found that a forty-second break spent viewing an urban roof garden could dramatically increase people's attention span when returning to a task afterwards.[1]

This doesn't mean you have to climb a mountain. I'm learning, especially now that I'm pregnant, to embrace gentler alfresco activities. While my husband surfs, I sketch seashells. Or we hang our hammocks between two trees in a national park and brainstorm big plans for our future. I've even found ways to work while 'nature bathing'—a Japanese practice where you immerse yourself in nature. When I was writing my last book, I spent three months working at picnic tables in various national parks across Australia, with my iPad plugged into a solar charger.

Nature has also taught me about patience. When we were backpacking across Costa Rica, I tasted the fruit of the langsat tree, which takes three years to ripen. For someone who has rushed their way through life in the past, I was in awe of this tiny fruit, which had waited so patiently to be ready. In its own way, nature has also taught me about second chances—watching forests recover from bush fires, greener and brighter than they were before they were desecrated. What greater role model could we have!

☐ THE BENEFITS OF ECOTHERAPY

Since my time in the rainforest, I've interviewed some incredible adventure lovers who admit they need a regular hit of nature to be happy, fulfilled and inspired. I'm always especially inspired when I talk to people who've purposefully built their lives to enable them to spend time in the wild.

I've interviewed the Creative Director of GoPro, who told me about the time he swam into an underwater canyon to 'dance' with humpback whales. I spoke to champion freediver William Trubridge, the first person to dive to 100metres unassisted, about how he thinks of freediving as a form of meditation. I tracked down adventurer Alyssa Azar, who became the youngest Australian to reach the summit of Everest, at the age of nineteen. She described the sound of ice cracking, as she scaled the hardest section of the climb in the pitch-black: 'Talk and image mean nothing in the mountains . . . the mountains always keep me humble.'

One of my most humbling interviews was with adventurer Alice Verral, who has hiked and biked 11,000km across Australia—despite having cerebral palsy. In Alice's case, her condition means she can't write or turn on a tap and she struggles to balance. However, despite her disability, she set herself an intimidating mission: to explore the most challenging national parks and rail trails in Australia, using a custom-built trike that she named 'Freedom.' 'When I finish university, I plan to travel the world,' said Alice. 'I want to see Africa, the Grand Canyon and the Amazon. It won't be easy, but I never give up. I want to show people that anyone, especially disabled people, can do whatever they set their mind to.'

⌒ When did you last step outside yourself, physically or mentally?

○ When did you last go somewhere just to breathe in the fresh air?

○ When did you last take off your shoes, stand in the grass and really feel it?

○ When did you last spend time in a place so naturally beautiful that it restored your faith in the world?

When it comes to ecotherapy, I've discovered that the healing power of nature is often amplified if you share it with like-minded people, although time alone is important too. With the internet, Facebook and event boards like Meetup, it's never been easier to find adventure buddies, even if you're a complete novice.

I'm a member of Intrepid Landcare—a landcare group for young people who undertake volunteer bush regeneration work across Australia. I also belong to OneWave, a not-for-profit organisation that aims to break down the stigma around mental health issues. Its founder, Grant, was diagnosed with bipolar disorder in his twenties, after a manic episode which left him hospitalised. In the aftermath, he discovered that surfing helped him to 'fight the funk' on his bad days; he felt most comfortable talking to his mates about his feelings when in the ocean. Now, every Friday morning at beaches across Australia, hundreds of people in fancy dress go surfing together (#flurofriday). They also work with hospitals, to include 'salt water therapy' in their mental health programs.

Depending where you live, you may not have a natural oasis on your doorstep. But even in the world's most built-up cities you can access a dose of nature, if you find the motivation. There is really no excuse to live your life in shades of grey instead of green.

Exploring nature has also helped me to shake the final shackles of my eating disorder and body issues. My husband and I go to nudist beaches on the weekend; and when we go surfing, I'll happily strip naked in a car park to change into my wetsuit.

When we were travelling, we spent a very memorable weekend at a clothing-optional camp in the middle of the Mojave Desert. I struck a business deal while sitting in a hot spring, naked except for a pair of sunglasses, sharing a plate of hummus and carrot sticks with a tech executive, a medical student and the CEO of an online shopping website.

To me, it's incredible that I can feel comfortable in these situations. During my starvation period, I did anything to avoid looking at my own body. But it just goes to show that you can overcome even the most crippling body hang-ups and change the story that you associate with your self-image—and, for some reason, it's much easier to do so when you're surrounded by nature's beauty rather than confined within a building

When I was in the Tarkine rainforest I experienced the true healing power of nature on a life-changing level. Until this point, I was still punishing my body, in a sense. I put it through it's paces during workouts and pushed it to it's limits without mercy. But in the depths of a forest I needed my body to be my ally, because injury, dehydration or exhaustion can all be deadly. As I hiked across the rainforest, I had a conversation with my body. I said that I was sorry and asked it to forgive me and to support me. Every morning before leaving camp, I taped up my blisters and massaged my muscles. I hadn't cared for my body in that way for a long time—and it was grateful.

On the final day of our trek through the Tarkine rainforest, I got my period for the first time in seven long years. It felt like an olive branch from my body—a symbol of trust, acceptance and recovery. Fast forward three years, and our baby was conceived in a national park on the edge of the beach during a camping trip. At the time I was so worried that I couldn't fall pregnant, and my doctor had suggested IVF treatment. There's an old proverb that says: Nature, time and patience are the three greatest physicians of all. My baby is proof of it's truth.

☐ HEALING RITUALS FOR YOUR NEXT OUTDOOR ADVENTURE

○ Ask for a safe path

Whenever we go hiking, as we enter a forest I silently greet Mother Nature or the 'elementals'—the creatures that some people believe are guardians of the trees. I tell them that we are there to worship the forest, that we won't take any more than we need from it, and I ask them to protect us and guide us as we go on our journey. It's a mindfulness exercise that encourages me to give thanks and feel grateful. It reminds me that I am lucky to be able to visit a place of such beauty.

○ Connect to past lives

Whenever I enter a forest, somewhere during the hike I close my eyes and think of all the people who have touched that trunk before me, over the years, decades and centuries since that tree emerged from the earth. I think of the children who have laughed in its branches, the mothers who may have birthed against its trunk, and the men who may have died beneath it. I take a moment to feel their energy stored in this natural life force and I leave an imprint of my energy behind me.

○ **Take a moon bath**
This is an ancient Ayurvedic practice, particularly recommended for people with a Pitta body type—a fiery nature that manifests in both body and mind. As the name suggests, this ritual involves lying outside in the moonlight, either clothed or naked. It's said that the lunar essence is symbolic of water—cool, fresh and flowing—and helps to calm anxiety and soothe anger or frustration. Many cultures also believe a woman's menstrual cycle should sync with the moon, so looking at the moon every night will help to regulate your period.

○ **Respect nature's rhythm**
One of my favourite memories of pregnancy is sitting on the floor of a forest trail with my husband sitting behind me, perfectly still and perfectly silent. There are few things as nourishing as napping in a hammock in the middle of a forest, away from the noise of the modern world. Take a moment to stop moving and tap into the rhythm of nature, which never hurries or rushes. Imagine your blood running slowly in your veins like a gentle stream. Imagine that your head is full of water. See it bubbling and swirling and then, like a lily pond, see the water become perfectly still.

◌ Don't look through a lens

I am as guilty as the next person of feeling the need to snap and post every moment. However, I've begun to purposefully bury my phone at the bottom of my backpack, so that I can't reach for it constantly when I'm exploring. For me, one of the most soothing parts of being outdoors is the sights, the sounds, the colours, the smells—and you can't capture that through a smartphone lens. One of my favourite things to do in the forest is stand at the bottom of a tree and just look up into its branches. There's something wonderful about the impermanence of a moment that you enjoy but don't capture.

THIRTEEN

Don't Wait Until You Need Resilience to Be Resilient

I am very resilient. That may come across as an arrogant thing to say, like calling yourself very pretty or very clever, but I know that I am from past experience. Resilience—an ability to adjust to misfortune—has allowed me to bound ahead from a lifetime of events that could have become setbacks, but instead became springboards. I'm not saying I'm invincible. I still fall down, get hurt, doubt myself and get punched in the face (metaphorically), by events I didn't see coming. But I always look forward, dust myself off and keep going.

Even when I catastrophise about my husband dying or my dad's cancer relapsing, within two minutes of the thoughts entering my head I'll have concocted a mental recovery plan: this is what I'll do, this is where I'll go, this is how I'll cope. I am so confident in my resilience that I truly believe there are few twists in life that could damage me beyond repair, emotionally. I read a quote by novelist Sophie Kinsella that sums my mindset up perfectly: There's no such thing as ruining your life. Life's a pretty resilient thing, it turns out.

Lately, resilience has become a hot topic, especially in the business world. Everyone wants know how to be more resilient, perhaps because we feel like the economy has become particularly unstable, due to financial uncertainty and political unrest. Psychologists struggle to study resilience, because whether you can be said to have it or not depends on your experiences. If you're never experienced real adversity, how can your resilience be accurately measured?

The American Psychological Association says resilience is an ongoing process that requires time and effort and engages people in taking a number of steps to accomplish.[1] So if, like me, your life has been a series of challenges then you're lucky—you've had practice! The trick, for everyone else, is to become resilient before you really need to be—and then practice.

Resilience is needed at every step on our life path, whether the road is flat or bumpy. I've discovered the hard way that it is not enough to practice my coping mechanisms when life is testing. I also have to maintain them when life feels easy.

When my husband and I first met, I was so 'busy' being happy that I stopped doing a lot of my self-care rituals. I'd neglected to meditate, journal and spend time in peaceful silence. A few months into our honeymoon period, when a career opportunity I was excited about fell through, I had no emotional buffer. I had stopped working on my resilience, which meant my defences were weakened. Think of it like fitness: if you stop training and eat junk food, you're not going to be able to run a marathon without a lot of pain and suffering.

☐ THE UNBREAKABLE TRUTH

When I was writing this chapter, I decided to crowdsource other people's experience of resilience. I sent an email to everyone in my contact book, no matter how well I knew them, with the subject line: Are You Resilient? to see what I would get back. I was interested to see how many people would put their hands up and, if so, how they believed they became resilient in the first place. Within two hours, I was astonished by the number of responses I received from people who believed they weren't born with resilience, but discovered how to be.

The first email I received was from an entrepreneur, who put his resilience down to an ability to problem-solve (he began installing car radios from his parents' garage at the age of fourteen, after watching his family struggling to pay their bills). I was floored by stories from people who'd been paralysed, lost parents and been made redundant from their dream jobs (one father, only seven days before Christmas). A lot of these people said they didn't consider themselves to have been born resilient—many were shy and reserved children who didn't respond well to conflict—yet as adults, they'd developed an amazing ability to recover emotionally.

A common thread among responses was the importance of self-care in building resilience. Many respondents spoke about how meditation and mindfulness had helped them. Some people's search for resilience had taken them across the world, including the amazing story of David, who lost his father when he was ten and then developed a profound stutter. To help his speech defect he discovered meditation and later travelled to China to study Chinese medicine, becoming one of a small number of ordained Taoists in the West (read more about his story on the website Wu Wei Wisdom).

Out of almost 100 emails, only one person believed they were 'naturally' resilient and had been born that way. The rest had become more resilient out of necessity, by nurturing the ability. The same coping mechanisms came up time and again: focus your energy on looking for solutions; search for problems you can solve, instead of concentrating on elements out of your control; don't compare yourself to other people (ego is an enemy of resilience); and above all, practise gratitude for what you do have.

One of the final responses came from Australian life coach, Lisa Cox, who has contributed to many of my articles before. At the age of 24, Lisa had a brain haemorrhage, similar to a stroke, later found to be caused by the strepto-coccus-A virus. She spent a year in hospital, during which she 'died' twice as her organs shut down. She underwent over a dozen operations including amputation of one leg, all her toes and nine fingertips. Although Lisa survived, her recovery was slow and painful.

Amazingly, it was gratitude that kept her going. 'That first year in the hospital was tough,' said Lisa. 'I don't remember all of it because I was either in a coma or under anaesthetic on an operating table. However, I do remember being grateful. Gratitude was and still is a choice for me. It is possible to be grateful amid the grief.' After her nine fingers were amputated, she focused on the fact she'd got to keep one thumb. After being told her leg would have to be amputated, she sat down and wrote a tongue-in-cheek list of the advantages of only having one leg (including a 50 percent discount on leg waxing and half-price reflexology). Her mantra is: My limb may have come off but my life will go on.

□ THE BUSINESS OF RESILIENCE

Entrepreneurs are the happiest people on the planet, according to a study[1] that examined more than 197,000 people in 70 countries. By its nature, running your own company requires an incredible amount of resilience—the ability to remain buoyant during slumps in sales, staff crises and competitors celebrating their victories.

In a blog post, Sir Richard Branson talked about resilience and its different stages. 'In the early days of business, everything you do is centred on surviving—something that takes great resilience to achieve,' he wrote. 'Then when you graduate to being an established business, resilience becomes the key to growing your success. And when you finally feel like you're solid and impactful, resiliency forms the glue that keeps you at the top of the game.'[1]

Although he was speaking about entrepreneurship, I think the sentiment applies to every life role. Take parenthood. In the early days of parenthood, everything you do is centred on surviving—something that takes great resilience to achieve. Then when you graduate to being an experienced parent, resilience becomes the key to growing your success. And when you finally feel like you're solid and impactful, resiliency forms the glue that keeps you at the top of the game.

You don't need to be an entrepreneur to learn from the resilience of start-up founders who, despite daily challenges, are so far managing to keep going—and enjoying it. A leader is constantly under pressure, emotionally and financially, to elevate not only themselves but their entire company.

So, how do they remain so resilient despite it all?

○ **They embrace their passions**
The founder of GoPro, Nick Woodman, has been dubbed the 'mad billionaire'—and he's pretty happy about it. He earned the titled because of his devil-may-care attitude and his love of adrenaline sports, which led him to create the iconic action camera. As Nick explains, 'I feel like, in a world where we all try to figure out our place and our purpose, your passions are one of your most obvious guides.' For you, this could mean turning a hobby into a business or simply finding ways to honour your hobbies, even when your schedule is frantic. Often when we're under stress, the extracurricular activities that make us happy take a back seat because we're too busy. But this is the time when you need an endorphin boost more than ever.

○ **They know their happiness triggers**
Tony Hsieh is the CEO of e-commerce store Zappos, which has been voted the happiest place to work in the world. In

his book Delivering Happiness, Tony shares the tricks he has used to harness a positive attitude. 'I made a list of the happiest periods in my life and I realised that none of them involved money,' he explains. 'I realised that building stuff and being creative and inventive made me happy. Connecting with a friend and talking through the entire night until the sun rose made me happy. Pickles made me happy.'

Your happiness triggers could be big or small: spending time out with a friend, having your favourite coffee on standby, visiting a park and lying on your back under a tree. It's comforting to remember how many of the things that make us happy cost very little (or nothing at all) because you realise that, whatever happens in your professional life, you can still access them any time.

○ **They set the scene**
As a Buddhist monk and founder of the meditation app Headspace, Andy Puddicombe designed the start-up's headquarters to orientate it towards happiness. In the main space, a wall of quotes reminds staff members to focus on kindness, and there's a tech-free 'silent room' where employees can go to work or meditate. The mindful entrepreneur learnt the importance of soothing surroundings when recovering from testicular cancer. 'I had the good fortune to be in a lovely environment to recover,' he says. 'I'd apply mindfulness to walking in the garden or doing my rehab exercises.'

Whether you work in an office or at home, take time to think about the look and feel of the space where you create. Make it vibrant or soothing, light and bright, and hang photos or quotes that inspire you. It can very easy these days to just put your laptop down anywhere, but our working environment can have a wonderful effect on our ability to stay calm and joyful.

○ **They hire positive influences**

The co-founder of Innocent Smoothies, Richard Reed, says he and two mates created the company with 'a view to create happiness.' Famous for their 'wackaging' (quirky packaging), they have never taken themselves too seriously. They were also careful to avoid toxic employees. 'We had a zero-cock policy,' says Richard. 'Don't employ any cocks, don't put up with any cocks. The vibe of the business to this day is that it's full of altruistic, ambitious people, so it's just an encouraging place to be.' Even if you work alone, this is worth considering. In times of stress, be careful who you confide in and who you spend your time with; be conscious of people who make you feel worse after meeting them. I do have friends who are prone to being dramatic. I still love them but they're not my first choice of confidant when I have a career crisis.

○ **They vary their experiences**

As the co-creator of TED Talks, Chris Anderson describes himself in his Twitter bio as 'A dreamer. Most days an optimist.' So what lessons has he learnt from curating the eighteen-minute speech platform? 'I think a lot of what people get from TED is the rediscovery of wonder,' he says. 'In talk after talk you see people who have done something or discovered something surprising, often at considerable effort, and the cumulative effect is to make you think that life has more possibilities than I'm used to thinking about.'

In my experience, stress can make us view life through a very small lens—our vision shrinks down to our problem; that is all we can think about and all we pay attention to. It's important to find ways to expand your vision again to all the other possibilities in life that are open to you and all the inspiring things people are doing. This could be as simple as binging on TED Talks, visiting a gallery you've never been to before, or going to a new cafe and people watching for an hour. Anything that reminds you there is always Option B.

☐ YOUR SOUL CONTRACT

I believe we all signed a contract before entering this life—to be a partner, carer, mother, teacher, storyteller, creative or any other role we are drawn to. I believe that, before our energy chose our body, we committed to a life purpose and to a contract embracing it. This belief has helped me to face and accept every struggle in my life, without feeling like a victim or wondering why it is happening to me. I chose this life path. I signed my soul contract. This is why I am here. I was created to cope with these circumstances. This reduces one of the side effects of trauma—feeling out of control—because I believe I made the choice to experience these circumstances. I signed my soul contract, not because I was forced to but because I wanted to.

I believe the one factor that's vital to everyone's resilience is trust—the trust that one day we'll be happier; the trust that tomorrow may be easier; the trust that we are capable of withstanding challenges even if it doesn't feel like it at the time. You've probably tapped into your soul's contract without even realising it—that unexplained sense of calmness you can access, even when the worst is happening; the ability you have to see the meaning in tragedy; the drive you have to keep going even, when something looks impossible.

During all my trials, although I've often wondered how I'd possibly get through them, I've also known I would get through them. That's an incredibly comforting belief, when you're surrounded by darkness.

When my husband and I started trying for a baby, I was commissioned to write an article about the realities of IVF treatment. The woman who generously agreed to share her story suffered from unexplained infertility and had just completed her fourth cycle of IVF treatment. The morning after our interview, she had a hospital appointment to find out if the latest round had been successful.

She spoke about the toughest challenges of her journey and how she stayed positive by listening to guided visualisation tapes and spending time with her friend's children. She told me her least favourite question is: How many more times will you try if this cycle fails? 'That's worse than asking a single woman if she's given up on getting married,' she said. 'It's worse because having a baby is out of my control. It's not up to me or even the doctors or medical process. Even when they put the eggs and sperm together, they can't say for definite that it will end up as a baby. It still needs a bit of magic. I haven't stopped believing in magic yet.'

A week later she emailed with an update—she was having a baby. She has signed a soul contract to be a mother and the struggle was part of her journey.

> If you can't hope for a better day,
> Just hope for another day.
> The universe with do the rest.

FOURTEEN

Heart Desires: That Unloving Feeling

When I was editor at Grazia magazine, we ran an amazing article by Australian blogger Eden Riley titled: I Tried to Un-love My Husband. In it she spoke about one of the toughest challenges in her life—when she was nine months pregnant and discovered her husband had cancer. 'Dave came home from hospital a broken man,' she blogged. 'There were nights when he'd be up vomiting, calling out for me. Then the baby would wake for a feed and I had to choose who to help.'

At the time, she also had a six-year-old son to take care of. 'I started to gradually pull away from my husband,' she recalled. 'I was so hurt that he got sick—though it was no fault of his. He was the only man I have ever truly loved. And now I was going to lose him. Over the next six months, I slowly built up walls, emotionally cutting off from him. If you don't care about things in life, nothing can hurt you . . . Soon I convinced myself that I would be okay alone.'

Thankfully, their story had a happy ending. Her husband recovered and their relationship rekindled. I read that article so many times I could almost recite it word for word. Although our stories weren't identical, I identified with Eden's journey on so many levels. I had never tried to 'un-love' my first husband when he had cancer. But after his death I did try to un-love everyone else who mattered to me, pushing them away, one by one.

The people I pushed away were innocent—my family, my friends, my future partners. These were people who had only ever supported and loved me. But that was the problem—I loved them back, deeply, which made me feel vulnerable. If they couldn't get near me, they couldn't hurt me. If they couldn't get near me, I couldn't see them get hurt either.

- When your life becomes stressful, do you reach out to loved ones or detach from them?
- Do you lean into love or reject it?
- Have you lashed out at someone you love, because of a trauma that has nothing to do with them?
- Have you chosen loneliness over vulnerability because, at the time, it felt safer?

On the internet, you'll find hundreds of blogs, posts and articles about 'how to fall out of love when you need to,' with people swapping tips for how to break free of unrequited love. But my love was requited. I was pushing away people who loved me deeply, people who supported me loyally and made my life fuller.

It sounds like a rom-com cliché—pushing away love because you're scared of getting hurt again. When I was young and began watching romantic movies, I remember asking myself: 'Why would anyone do that? Why would you ever be mean to someone you love?' As an adult, I get it! It's pure self-preservation.

I picked a fight with my husband a week before he died, because I caught him smoking in the garden shed. It was a good excuse to be angry. I could leave him emotionally, before he left me. I said some terrible things to my family in the early days of my widowhood. I was angry and desolate, so lashed out at them, blamed them and abused them. I ignored phone calls from my friends—for years.

My mum has admitted that in the first few years after I was widowed I became harsh and cold. I made any excuse not to attend family occasions or I'd arrive withdrawn and hungover. I am a stubborn person, so I found it surprisingly easy to un-love my loved ones. In retrospect, it was scary how quickly I could switch off my feelings, when I decided to.

In hindsight, my aversion to love began even before I was widowed. The first bricks in my walls went up when I stopped eating and realised the people closest to me were most likely to uncover my secret. I also knew how much pain my condition caused them, and I didn't want to see it in their eyes when they looked at me. More than anything, I felt incredibly angry—at my loved ones, at strangers, at anyone I could use as a target. I've seen similar reactions in other people.

One of my friends struggled for nearly ten years to have a baby, before welcoming a beautiful little girl via adoption. During the period when she and her husband were trying to conceive, she became increasingly angry—at her husband, her family, the universe and at every single couple who had conceived a baby easily. She once yelled at a pregnant woman on a bus, who was talking to her friend about how it only took her one month to fall pregnant!

I once interviewed a father whose twenty-year-old daughter died in a plane crash. I remember being struck by the lack of emotion and affection he voiced towards his daughter, despite family videos showing how close they were. I recognised the symptoms—the robotic tone of his voice; the odd anger he felt towards another daughter who wasn't on the flight; the way he quickly changed the subject when I encouraged him to recall happy memories.

The problem with forcing yourself to fall out of love is that emotion—that passion, that fire—has to go somewhere. I recently read a blog post on the website Quora written by a guy who tried to fall out of love with his ex-girlfriend, after she ended their relationship. If only I'd read it sooner. 'Love, in the end, is just another form of energy,' he wrote. 'If there's something about energy you ought to know it's that it isn't destroyed, only altered. All of that love you have converts into something else. Don't follow my past self's example and displace your love by letting it turn into hatred.'

How do you learn to re-love after tragedy? How do you re-enter the world after a period of solitary confinement? If my life was a rom-com, the remedy to my love sickness would be a man who made it impossible to resist him. But I think the twist in my love story is even better. In the end, it was a group of women who taught me to re-love again.

☐ THE WOMEN WHO TAUGHT ME TO LOVE

My first mentor in love was Marisa, who I met at a yoga studio in Bondi Beach, a few months after moving to Australia. During my first class she came up and welcomed me, even though she was just another student. She hugged me—really hugged me. 'You seemed kind of shocked that I had done it,' she recalls. 'You had this strange look on your face afterwards, like you weren't sure what had just happened.'

She told me that on the following weekend she was getting married—for the third time and to the same man. As Marisa is from America and her husband is from Australia, they decided to have a series of celebrations: a ceremony at New York City hall with just her parents; a party on an organic farm with friends and family; and then another big lunch on the edge of Sydney Harbour.

It seemed so amazing to me—the idea of celebrating love so indulgently. After my dad got sick and then my husband died, I stopped celebrating birthdays, let alone Valentine's Day and anniversaries. When I got married for the second time, I only invited four people to the registry office. Instead of buying something new, I wore the dress I'd last worn to my husband's funeral. Even that felt uncomfortably showy.

Yet here was Marisa—a smart, educated woman who was celebrating love unashamedly and didn't see love as a disability. After the third wedding, the happy couple and their in-laws were even going away on a 'familymoon' together. I remember I felt nervous for her; I felt like I needed to warn her, although I didn't know what I was warning her about. Five years on, Marisa is joyfully married and has become an incredible friend and a role model to me.

Over the next few years, other significant women came into my world and helped me to soften my emotional barriers. My friend Avis—an incredible social entre-preneur— introduced me to the idea that you can choose who to fall in love with, rather than love being a passive action that is out of our control. (There's a great TED Talk by Mandy Len Catron that touches on this topic).

On the journey back to lovingness, I spent hours listening to meditation tracks by Sister Jayanti, European Director of the Brahma Kumaris World Spiritual. She talks about the healing power of love and how it creates and sustains human relationships.

My life coach was also an important mentor in helping me to reunite with my family. When I decided to fly back to England for the first time in three years, I was nervous about spending so much time with my parents. I suspected that I might self-sabotage the trip, to push them away again. 'Imagine that this may be the last time you'll ever see them,' said Eli. 'Imagine that when you get back on the plane, that will be their last memory of you. How would you want to spend your last two weeks together?' You might think that, given my history, this reminder of mortality would raise my barriers higher but, during that visit, we bonded in a way we hadn't for a decade, rediscovering the people we'd become since I pushed them away.

I still have moments where love makes me feel incredibly vulnerable. But I am proud that, today, I love wholeheartedly with clear intention. When I choose to love someone, I do it with complete devotion, not because love has swept me away but because I've chosen to dive into the ocean. By the time I hiked into the rainforest, I could fall in love without question. By the time I welcomed my daughter into my body, I could connect with her devotedly, without hesitation.

After years as an island, I didn't fall in love—I chose it. And to choose love feels very different to not feeling like you're in control of it. One of my favourite quotes is from The Fault in Our Stars, a book by John Green which tells the story of two teenage cancer patients who are in love with each other. I have one of the lines on a poster above my desk: You don't get to choose if you get hurt in this world . . . but you do have some say in who hurts you. I like my choices.

☐ WOMAN OR WARRIOR?

Are your coping mechanisms typically masculine or feminine? As a woman, is your female or male energy dominant? In times of stress or when you feel tested, what gender is your behaviour? Do you nurture yourself with care, tenderness and compassion? Or do you charge onwards like a warrior, fighting your way to a perceived finishing line?

There is not necessarily a right or wrong answer here. But the gender energy of your coping mechanisms will have an effect on how you form relationships, recover from emotional injury and feel within your body, or so I discovered.

In the modern age, a lot of women have fallen into a traditionally male way of coping, recovering or succeeding. I get it. I did it! After my husband died, I shut my feminine energy in a box, because it seemed detrimental to me—far too vulnerable and far too breakable. I didn't want traits like compassion and empathy slowing me down. I wanted to be a survivor, a fighter, a warrior. I needed to be strong because I was angry.

My masculine dominance also meant I refused to take help from anyone, because I could provide for myself, or so I thought. But surviving is exhausting, especially when you only have yourself to rely on. It didn't only take an emotional toll on my mind, but also had an incredible physical effect on my body.

Interestingly, all of my physical injuries were on the left side of my body—the side of the body that is often regarded as the feminine side, the 'receiving' side. Within a period of six months I injured my left ankle, my left knee, my left shoulder, and constantly felt tension down the left side of my neck. I now know this can mean there are issues with unbalanced energy in your body.

As someone who has been on a journey of rejecting their feminine energy and then re-finding it (through a lot of healing), I'm now always interested to watch how other women, particularly those with A-type personalities and incredible self-discipline, cope with testing situations—especially the gender of energy they call on.

Sometimes the world can feel harsh and to survive it can feel necessary to toughen, to harden and wrap yourself in a suit of armor. There is nothing wrong, in the short term, in drawing on typically male tendencies (fighting, striving, providing), to muscle your way through a situation but it can have an uncomfortable side effect.

In the early years after I was widowed, my masculine dominance helped me to stay standing, keep functioning, take charge and move forward—but I was really only surviving. I was also totally and utterly exhausted, constantly.

There is a beautiful quote by Hay House author and spiritual teacher Gabby Bernstein. 'Fear is a sure sign you've been relying on your own strength,' she says. When I heard this statement during Gabby's 9-week Spirit Junkie program which I completed (and highly recommend!) it felt like an epiphany. That is why I always felt so tired. That is why I always felt so drained. That is why I often felt so scared.

I was relying on my own strength, constantly pulling, dragging and clawing myself back up, instead of allowing myself to be lifted by the people who loved me.

To step into my feminine essence again, I needed to embrace her unique strengths—softness, flexibility, compassion and an ability to receive. I also needed to accept that this didn't make me weak, in fact quite the opposite.

Not long after completing Gabby's course I had an unforgettable dream (after sleeping with a piece of Selenite under my pillow—a crystal that promotes angel guidance).

I dreamt that I was in the midst of a healing session where a stranger laid their hands on my back—my left, feminine side—and I felt incredible energy flow through me. 'You've done so well, considering you've been broken,' the stranger said, touching my left arm which, in my dream, I couldn't move, 'But now it's time for you to heal so you can really fly.'

So, I embarked on a mission to soften, in the best way possible.

I learnt to honour my feminine energy by subtle methods at first. It may sound like a cliché, but it's one of the reasons I began to change my dress sense. I bought the floatiest, most colourful trousers in the shop—the ones I always wanted to buy but flicked past for more practical options. I stopped tying my hair in a ponytail for yoga and began plaiting it or wearing it lose. Whenever I did it I felt instantly softer.

To encourage a nurturing energy, I also followed an Ayurvedic Vata diet for six months—a healing eating plan that revolves around warm, wet, nurturing food and aims to balance out people with rough, dry, cold dispositions. I bought candles and coconut shampoo and rediscovered my sensuality. I let my body rest when it needed to and began to learn to accept help (I am still not very good at this but I am trying).

I also found rituals that honored my womanliness, including my internal organs. Whenever I'm in a yoga class and we reach the final pose—Savasana—instead of lying flat with my arms by my sides, I place my palms over my ovaries and imagine white, glowing light flooding my sexual organs. When I meditate, I sit cross-legged and fold my hands in my lap, imagining that I'm cradling my own womb within my palms. When I was trying for a baby, my spiritual healer told me to visualise my uterus as a warm, soft, inviting pillow, where the soul of my child could land comfortably and safely.

If you feel like you hold tension in your sacral chakra—the chakra below your bellybutton which is associated with your sex organs—then I recommend you buy a Tibetan singing bowl. For centuries, the Tibetan people have practised sound healing with this musical instrument. The resonance produced by these bowls is believed to improve immune function, lower blood pressure, soothe pain and reduce stress levels. Before bed, especially if I want to shake my day off, so I can connect with my husband, I hold my singing bowl in front of my uterus and chime it, imagining my whole body softening.

It reminds me of the quote from the spiritual teacher Yogi Bhagani, who first introduced Kundalini yoga to the United States, He says, 'If a woman sits with folded hands in her lap for a few minutes every day, and feels she is a container so vast that she contains the whole universe, she will never feel weak or have any problems.'

This doesn't mean I can't harness my kick-arse warrior power when I need it. I still draw on my masculine energy when I need him in the short term—when I need to take action quickly to deal with a combative situation. But I've found that I feel more at ease in my feminine energy. I walk slowly, I think softly and I approach life with more tenderness.

After I wrote a blog post about my quest to soften for the wellness website The Glow (which included mention of my missing period) I received an incredible amount of emails and social media messages from women, including friends, who all shared the same problem—high-achieving, go-getting women with incredible jobs, busy lives, ambitious plans. And no menstrual cycle.

It's an epidemic that we're not talking about openly enough. How a generation of warrior women are so busy, so ambitious, so daring and driven they're disconnecting from their womanly emotions—and functions. Stress is a major cause of infertility and an increasing number of women suffer from The Female Athlete Triad (a syndrome that typically afflicts female athletes whose periods stop due to inadequate nutrition, low bone mass and overexertion).

Many of the women who wrote to me could pinpoint the milestone when their menstrual cycle stopped—when they started a new stressful job, when their relationship broke down, when their parent got sick. When they stopped just 'being' and started having to fight to survive each day.

Next time you're placed in a stressful situation, examine your coping mechanisms.

Is your masculine or feminine energy dominant? There isn't really a right or wrong answer. I know women who are capable of attacking their careers and personal lives with raw male energy and no negative side effects. I also know men whose feminine energy shines out of them. But for me, personally, I was ready to let down my guard.

The duality of our male and female energies enables us to fulfil all the roles in our lives—mothers, lovers, survivors, warriors and creators. But when our gender energies are out of balance (or when one is ignored completely), we can become capable but uncaring, strong but rigid, courageous but cold. In the schoolyard being called 'soft' can be seen as an insult. For me, it's been the secret to enjoying life, rather than enduring it. Is it time you softened up?

☐ SOFTENING STRATEGIES FOR WHEN YOU FEEL YOURSELF HARDENING

☐ Spend time around feminine energy. Go to a yoga class full or women, sign up to an all-female wellbeing retreat or invite your most feminine friend, that one who is incredibly at peace with herself, to spend time with you.

☐ Massage your belly with coconut oil after having a shower. Don't rush to get your clothes on, take time to pamper and nurture yourself.

☐ Treat yourself to a piece of rose quartz crystal—the crystal thought to heal heartache. Sleep with it under your pillow or, as I did for years, carry a small piece in the cup of your bra.

☐ Put on your floatiest clothing and dance. I've never done a single ballet class but, when I'm alone in the house, I put on music and unleash my inner ballerina.

☐ Sit on a patch of grass under a tree on a soft blanket. Hold a cup of tea in your hands and feel the warm glow sweep from your palms through your body.

☐ Read a romantic novel or watch a soppy film. Allow yourself to feel for the characters, even though it's fictional. Let your tears flow if they need to.

☐ Spend time away from your partner, just long enough so you miss them.

☐ Spend time around children—listen to them, make eye contact, have a conversation even if it's unspoken.

☐ Make love.

☐ Repeat this mantra: I expand into love, joy and kindness. By doing so, I inspire others to do the same.

FIFTEEN

Goodbye for Now: Love and Long-Distance Love

When I was little, my dad would travel a lot. Working as a marine engineer, he would go to countries I couldn't even pronounce, returning with presents for me and my sister— tapestries of pyramids, exotic candy and the complimentary toiletry bags they give out on aeroplanes. As a child, I didn't realise that he often worked in war-torn countries or how dangerous his job could be. When he arrived home early from Mozambique, I was so excited to see my daddy I didn't notice the bandages around both his wrists. He'd been involved in a car crash in which three people had died. He'd caught the first flight home with shards of glass still stuck in his arms, and by the time he landed in Heathrow they were septic. As soon as he was healed, he was off again.

This was before the internet when the only form of contact was a long-distance phone call once a week, on a crackling line that meant we could barely hear each other.

There was no Skype and no FaceTime; we didn't even have a mobile number through which to contact him, as he'd often be working offshore on oil rigs. As a child, I would lie awake wondering where my daddy was and whether he was thinking of us. My mum was amazing but the energy in our house changed every time he was away. I felt disconnected and missed him terribly. And then one night my mum taught me about the 'golden thread.'

She told me that everyone who loves each other is joined by a golden thread, running between the centres of their hearts. No matter how far away my dad was, this sparkling piece of string would join us together, unbreakable and as long as it needed to be. If I looked really, really hard I could see it. Before going to sleep, she told me to mentally follow the thread—from my heart, out of our house, down our street, along the highway, across oceans, up mountains and through jungles, until it reached my dad's hotel room. I would imagine the golden thread trailing up the leg of his bed, along his mattress and to his chest. It joined us; heart to heart and soul to soul.

It's a visualisation technique that I still use as an adult. I've imagined a golden thread leading from my heart to my dad's hospital bed, from my heart to my first husband's coffin, from my heart to my mum's on the other side of the world. Even now, if my husband has to work late I'll imagine it winding into his office along the electricity cables. I've explained the golden thread to my friend's children when Mummy and Daddy no longer live together, to teenagers whose best friend is in a different state, and to gap year backpackers who are missing boyfriends back home. On the day I had my twelve-week ultrasound, I got an envelope in the mail with a British postmark. It contained a single piece of golden thread from my mum, to remind me that she was with me.

This isn't the only way I've used visualisation to deal with separation. Whenever people hear that I live 15,000 miles from my parents they ask, 'But don't you miss them?' Of course I do! But since emigrating, I've developed a toolkit of methods to maintain our connection and help me feel close to them. When I meditate, I visualise that I'm sitting in my parents' garden under their apple tree, listening to my mum singing to the radio in the kitchen. After I went through a messy break-up, my dad would FaceTime me and talk me through a guided meditation—both of us sitting on opposite sides of the planet, connected by his calming words and positive affirmations.

In Australia, over 1.1 million children have a natural parent living elsewhere from them.[1] The rates of divorce are rising, but it's also not uncommon for one parent to be pulled away for work, flying in and flying out for weekends or living away for months at a time. As adults, we don't escape the strains of separation either, with long-distance romances and an increasing number of millennials living in a different country to where they were born.

Separation can be physical, with two people pulled apart by distance. It can also be emotional, with two people pulled apart by changing circumstances (two best friends still live in the same postcode, but one gets married while the other remains single). As I enter my first year of marriage and prepare to welcome our baby, my best friend is single and infertile. Your love for each other has not changed but your life paths have taken one of you on a detour in another direction.

In the French language, they don't really say 'I miss you.' Instead they use the phrase tu me manques, which means 'you are missing from me.' It's a feeling most of us can identify with, whether you were a child of divorce, you moved house a lot when you were young, you've chosen to move countries as an adult or—through death or illness—your physical connection with a person has been cut, temporarily or forever.

Research shows that experiencing separation in our younger years can make it harder to commit to relationships as an adult; even in our twenties and thirties, separation can lead to anxiety, depression and a sense of isolation. In adults, loneliness increases the risk of depression, alcoholism and even suicide.

So how can you miss someone, without missing part of yourself?

A Writing Exercise:
WHAT DOES IT FEEL LIKE TO MISS SOMEONE?

Spend five minutes writing (without taking the tip of
your pen or pencil off the paper) about what the sense of
missing someone means to you. How would you describe
the feeling of missing someone to a person who has never
felt it? What is your experience of missing someone and
how does it feel in your body?

☐ THE SHAPES OF SEPARATION

I am the first to admit that I suffer from separation anxiety,
when it comes to my current relationship. It's partly because
I tend to catastrophise that something terrible will happen
to him when I'm not with him (widowhood does that to
you!) but also because, like most human beings, my self-
esteem is more fragile than I like to admit. Every time my
husband works late or chooses to go surfing without me,
a little voice in my head says, 'Shouldn't he want to be
with you?' It's illogical because I know—we all know—that
it's unhealthy for two people to spend every moment of
their day together. We all know that relationships ebb and
flow, come and go. Yet it can still feel uncomfortable when

someone we love is away from us—especially if they have made the choice to do so.

During my career, I've seen separation in many different shapes and forms. After the terrible Japanese earthquake and tsunami in 2011, I interviewed a mother whose five-year-old daughter was, at the time, missing in the rubble. Unsurprisingly, she was utterly inconsolable. However, I've also seen the same level of grief in a couple saying goodbye to each other at an airport departure gate. My friend Jo, who is in her third trimester of pregnancy, recently discovered that her best friend—and her son's godmother—was moving across the country to Queensland. After her friend broke the news, she sobbed on and off for an entire week. 'My husband couldn't believe how much it affected me,' she said. 'I was selfishly angry at my friend. She was the one who was meant to be there for me and now she was leaving, when I needed her most.'

Separation can sting, whether it's a romantic, platonic, paternal or maternal relationship. So it's important to acknowledge and 'treat' the condition. It can be shocking how much separation can affect us, especially if (like me) you consider you are a strong, independent woman.

When I was 22 and living in London, one of my friends was thrown into a long-distance relationship when her banker boyfriend was transferred to Dubai. I tried to comfort her one evening as she sobbed, 'It's okay for you Amy, your husband died. My boyfriend chose to leave me.' It might sound insensitive but I knew exactly what she meant. I don't think her grief was any less painful than mine, just because her partner was still alive.

You may not think you've experienced separation because you're not a child of divorce, but it takes many shapes and can be more subtle than a parent packing a suitcase. A fear of separation can begin when you're the last kid waiting at the school gate; when you're separated from a parent because of illness; when you're sent to a different school from your friends. There is new evidence to suggest that separating a newborn baby from their mother immediately after birth, even for a short period, increases their stress levels considerably and can have a lasting impact on their ability to bond[1].

This doesn't mean we should avoid or fear separation. I can't follow my husband to the office every day or ban him from undertaking extracurricular activities without me—nor would I want to. For all of us, separation is part of our lives but it doesn't have to be a situation that we dread.

Today, I acknowledge that a large part of my separation anxiety stems from the fear I had that each time I left my first husband, even just to buy a bottle of milk, he might be dead when I got home. That's an understandable fear, but it doesn't need to impact on my current relationship.

Your trigger might be less obvious than widowhood and could take some soul-searching or professional guidance to identify. But it's worth it. Understanding where your fear of separation comes from can help you to make peace with being apart, enabling you to go the distance with the people you love.

☐ THE ART OF NON-ATTACHMENT

In my journey of love and loss, one of the biggest things that helped me is reading about—and attempting to practise—the spiritual concept of non-attachment. I am the first to admit I am nowhere near nailing it! But just attempting to come close has helped me to deal with the emotions that surround separation and the fear that I might be separated from someone I love in the future.

The art of non-attachment (or detachment) is taught in Buddhism and Hinduism. It is difficult to understand, especially in a world where we place such high value on ownership. There are some brilliant books that cover the subject (Teachings on Love by Thich Nhat Hanh and Dare to Live by Miriam Subirana). To paraphrase their work and express their message as simply as possible: nothing in life is permanent, so to avoid having to let go, we should never cling to anyone or anything in the first place.

That can sound harsh and cold when you first begin to explore it. In the Western world, we are taught that love means attaching yourself to another person—two becomes one, bound together forever. As women, we're conditioned to say things like, I can't stop thinking about him or I only worry because I care. The signs of true love are similar to sickness: loss of appetite, sleep and concentration. But what if we could love as deeply without the uncomfortable side effects?

Is it really a good thing to say we can't stop thinking about someone? To stare out of a rainy window fantasising about a person when we can't be near them? In Miriam Subirana words: We know we are attached when we begin to think about someone or something when they are not present and there is no need to think about them.

This goes against the all-consuming idea of love we see in movies. But deep down, it's a much more sustainable concept of love and desire.

- Can you imagine saying goodbye without any negative emotion?
- Can you imagine, in the gap between seeing someone, feeling light, bright and contented?

This doesn't mean you don't love the person you're away from and you can still be overjoyed to see them again. But instead of counting down the moments until you're back together, pining and moping, you can live in the present and use your energy to fill that time with self-care, new experiences and magic moments. Then when you reunite with your loved one, you will only have positive stories, so that your time apart has the same value as your time together.

It seems like some people are better at this than others and I do think your background has a part to play. My husband has never studied detachment, yet he naturally practises it. When we are together he dotes on me, but the moment he goes to work it's like he presses a pause button. Generally, he doesn't think about me again unless I phone him, unless he needs to ask me a question or he has a practical reason to think about me.

You could say this is unromantic, but it enables him to fulfil his purpose at work. And it makes him a better partner because, when we are together, he is able to be 100 percent present and devoted, because he hasn't drained his emotional resources worrying about me when we're apart.

This doesn't mean he doesn't love me; he loves his job and his hobbies and doesn't let attachment block the flow of his productivity or enjoyment.

☐ ATTACHMENT IS LOVE + PAIN DETACHMENT IS PURE LOVE

This way of thinking takes practice because, ever since childhood, attachment and love have gone hand in hand for most of us. In his book The 7 Myths about Love . . . Actually, author Mike George says it begins when we are children and our favourite toy is lost or broken: You know the pain of sorrow. Your heart broke, briefly. Your heart was attached to the toy and when the toy was broken it seemed like your heart was also broken. We are held back by the belief that to be happy, confident, fulfilled or worthwhile we need one person—or in this case an object—near us, always.

Part of my exploration of detachment has been learning not to become overly attached to struggles that my loved ones are going through. A lot of us worry about something happening to someone we love, whether it's sickness, professional disappointment or some other kind of struggle. Detachment teaches you to be sympathetic and empathetic, without owning their situation.

Mike George uses the example of doctors, surgeons and nurses who are trained to detach from patients, so they can be affective caregivers. If my husband has a bad day at work I am sympathetic, but I remind myself that, just because he is stressed, I don't need to adopt that emotion. I can maintain my own happiness while supporting him through a bad patch.

When I worry about my dad's cancer returning I remind myself, 'This is not your illness. This is not happening to your body.' If his cancer does ever return, I hope that I can support him and hold space for him, without sacrificing my entire self to a battle that is not mine to fight.

Think about it in terms of your own life. If your best friend is sad you can be empathetic, but do you have to be sad for them? If your parent is ill, do you have to suffer? If your partner dies, is your life over too?

A big part of detachment comes down to ownership— or lack of it. Instead of thinking of a person as yours (my child, my partner), think of yourself as their temporary guardian. You can regard it as an honour to care for their wellbeing and to bring them joy and happiness, but know that you don't own them. All relationships are temporary, even if they last a lifetime.

To quote my spiritual healer: On the journey of life, different people will spend time in your train carriage and then get off again. The art of detachment comes down to being able to wave goodbye, with nothing but gratitude for the time that you've spent in tandem.

For me, detachment is an ongoing experiment and I will continue to read as much as I can, to better understand it. This doesn't just apply to people but also attachment to things and situations. For now, I try to implement it as best as I can, reminding myself to detach every time my husband packs up his car for a work trip, or I wave goodbye to my parents at the airport departure gate.

Personally, I don't always get it right. I go through stages where I become overly attached to people, to projects, to expectations and begin to lose myself. But eventually I rediscover my equilibrium. I have a mantra that I fall back on, whenever I feel separation anxiety emerging: I am safe, I am whole. I am everything I need.

We all are.

☐ UN-FRIENDING NEGATIVE FEELINGS

When I was thirty, I accidentally deleted every digital photograph I had ever taken. This included all photographic evidence of my university days, my backpacking adventures and family gatherings during my twenties. It also included every photograph I'd taken of my first husband, including our wedding and the surf trip we took after we learnt he had three months to live.

I have no-one else to blame but myself for my digital deletion. The previous September, after my last relationship had broken down, my ex-partner and I agreed that he would get 'custody' of our shared laptop. As all my files were stored on the computer, I arranged for him to transfer more than 4,500 photographs onto an external hard drive. In hindsight, I should have checked to make sure all of my photographs were there, but instead I saw a folder marked 'Amy's Pics' and made an incorrect assumption. I only realised my error twelve months later, when I was looking for a photo to accompany an article. I plugged in the hard drive, clicked on the folder . . . and it was empty.

In an age where we snap, pap and selfie every tiny life occurrence, it's a strange feeling to not have photographic evidence of the toughest years of your life. The only pictures I had left were those taken before my 21st birthday, mostly out of focus and taken with a series of cheap disposable cameras. Apart from that, every snapshot taken between the ages of 21 and 29 was a distant memory. Yet to my surprise I didn't cry, when I realised I would no longer have these memory prompts at my disposal. In fact, as the weeks went on, I felt an odd sense of relief and lightness, even though everyone kept telling me that I must be devastated.

At that time, I was still having fortnightly appointments with my psychotherapist. When I emailed her in a panic about my mistake, instead of being sympathetic she was actually happy for me. 'One of the most powerful processes of grief or disappointment is the fact that our memories fade with time; but digital evidence can keep us frozen in a period,' she said. 'That series of pictures taken on a wonderful holiday can become weapons in the hands of our inner critic. We can glorify who we were, who others were, and the 'perfect' life we led before a loss or hardship.'

In the digital age, grief has never been so complicated. We live in an era where all of our lives are constantly on show in high definition. But a digital footprint can be both a comfort and a hindrance, when you're the person left behind with a hard drive full of visual reminders.

It's not just photographs that keep a person's memory alive—vividly. Modern mourners also have the social media ghost to contend with, thanks to anniversary reminders from Facebook, last words on Twitter and remembrance sites like Gonetoosoon. The way we grieve has never been more public or high tech but is this really a good thing? There's an argument that part of the grieving process is the natural erosion of memories, and that digital evidence could stop us from moving on and healing.

Every person grieves differently and, for some, the use of technology boosts their emotional wellbeing. A few years ago an American father, whose six-week-old daughter had died of a liver condition, posted a plea on Reddit asking whether anyone could photoshop a photograph of his little girl. 'Since she was in hospital her whole life, we were never able to get a photograph of her without tubes,' wrote Nathan Steffel. 'Can anyone remove the tubes from the photo for us?' After just two days, his post had received more than 2,500 comments and Nathan had received hundreds of photoshopped versions of the picture, with the tubes removed and different backgrounds.

For other mourners, having a stockpile of reminders can be detrimental—and addictive. 'It's like lugging around a memory box wherever you go,' says my friend Francesca, who lost her older brother to leukaemia eight months ago. 'I have all these emotional triggers at the touch of an iPhone and, if I'm having a low moment, I'll Google my brother's name and feed my grief. It's almost addictive, scouring tweets and photos, feeling increasingly sorry for myself.'

Another friend Lucy, who lost her boyfriend in a motor-cycle accident, says the internet can be both comforting and tortuous. The morning after Martin's death she wrote on his public Facebook wall: I want you back. It was the only way she knew of reaching out. 'When I went back to work a few weeks after the funeral, the first message that popped up in my inbox was from Martin,' said Lucy. 'For two stunned seconds I thought he was alive, then I realised it was just an automatic message telling me that an email I'd sent him had been deleted without being read, because the company he worked for had disabled his account. I exploded into tears; it all seemed so final.'

She also logged onto her boyfriend's Facebook page after his death, after guessing his password. 'I read messages he'd sent to other girls that were thankfully cheeky rather than incriminating,' she said. 'It was also hard when girls I'd never heard of posted tribute messages on his Facebook wall. For a while I became obsessed with checking his Facebook page, until I eventually deleted my own account, as it all became too much.'

You don't need to have suffered a bereavement to identify. Although grief is associated with death, intense feelings of shock and sorrow can be triggered by many things—a friend turning on you, a partner betraying you, or someone you love lying to you. If you've ever lost hours looking at photos of an ex-partner, stalked someone's Facebook feed or reread old text messages or emails sent during a honeymoon period or after a break-up, you'll know it's not always healthy to binge on the past.

The problem with a digital legacy is that it's not always an accurate reflection of the entire picture. The last thing my husband posted on Facebook was a photograph taken on our wedding day. He's standing at the altar having just placed a ring on my finger, punching the air in triumph and whooping with joy. What you can't see is the pain he is hiding or the fact that his pockets are filled with steroid tablets, to try and stop the tumour in his brain swelling.

I'm not saying that everyone should delete their hard drive. For me, it was a happy mistake that enabled me to move forwards. When a song on the radio reminded me of my first husband, I was no longer tempted to spend an entire afternoon poring over old photographs of us. When I was having a 'fat' day, I couldn't look back at photos of my seventeen-year-old self in a bikini and wish I still had the figure of a teenager.

It made me more conscious of the effect that technology can have on the grieving process—both positive and negative. I unfriended my dead husband on Facebook and now have no idea if his account is still active. I only have five photographs of him which I found attached to an old email. I'm sure that I could gather more photos if I contacted people from our past, but I don't feel the need.

Today, I have selective amnesia when it comes to that period in my life, but I'm not going to use technology to fill in the blanks for me. I can't remember the exact location where my husband was buried. I can't remember the name of his doctor. I can't remember the last thing we ever said to each other. Some things are best forgotten for a reason.

☐ HOW TO LOSE SOMEONE YOU LOVE—WITHOUT LOSING YOURSELF

◌ **Control your inner catastrophist**
It is easy, when you've been to a dark place, to let your mind stray there again, especially if you're faced with certain triggers. But you always have a choice about whether to go there, or to let logic override it. If my husband is late

home from work and he doesn't answer his phone, my mind can quickly and dramatically spiral ('He's dead. It's over!'). When I see a missed call from my dad in the middle of the night I panic ('He's relapsed!'), even though I know he has a habit of accidentally calling me. In the past, I have been reduced to a sobbing, shaking ball on the floor, but my life coach has taught me to stop and regroup myself. 'What's more likely to be true?' I ask myself. 'What is more like to have happened?' I've also found that it helps to pause and breathe before reacting, before calling my husband fifty more times or phoning my sister in a panic. Don't panic until you have concrete evidence to warrant it.

⊂ **Cover your calendar**
It can be hard when anniversaries and birthdays come around, but does it really have to be? Do you have to feel worse today because it's exactly two years since a person departed? Or because this would have been the day you were due to get married? After my husband died, I realised that if I mourned every anniversary, every single year, I'd be in a constant cycle of bereavement—the date we met, the date we got engaged, the date his cancer was declared terminal. Ask yourself why you should feel any different today than yesterday? If you couldn't see a calendar and didn't know the date, would you feel any different today? This doesn't mean you can't commemorate an anniversary by doing something special if it serves you, but don't collapse emotionally just because other people tell you that 'today must be really hard for you.'

○ Looks still matter

When my husband was sick, I cut my long, blonde hair into a pixie cut and dyed it dark brown. It didn't suit me in the slightest, but it felt disrespectful to spend any time on my appearance. I remember the outfit I was wearing on the day he died—a brown knitted dress I would never have dreamed of wearing pre-cancer. Over the next few years, I felt guilty spending any time or money on my appearance. Then one day my psychotherapist gave me homework: to go home and paint my toenails in rainbow colours. I chose pink, orange and turquoise. I called them my 'happy toes,' because I smiled every time I saw them at yoga. The following January, for my New Year's Resolution I decided to stop wearing black yoga pants. It was a symbolic gesture—every time I put on a pair of bright, colourful pants I was allowing myself to celebrate life again. Today my hair is long, blonde, natural and flowing. My wardrobe is bright, colourful, quirky and comfortable. More than anything, it makes me smile.

○ Take comfort in strangers

I rely on the energy of strangers to uplift me on a daily basis, especially as my family live so far away: an old man giving me a thumbs up when I'm jogging; a morning greeting from the owner of a coffee shop I go to daily; a conversation with another chai tea drinker who is reading a magazine I write for. All of these interactions give my day meaning and give me a sense of belonging. Often they don't just happen—I seek out these interactions and I'm purposefully open to them. When you're sitting in a cafe, take a few moments to look around and smile at anyone who catches your eye. Go to the same places, so you can build a rapport with other regulars. Carry a prop! Before I was pregnant, I used to skateboard to everything—including work meetings—partly because I love it, but also because it's such a good conversation starter. I know people who wear bright costume jewellery or carry a book for the same reason.

○ **Save yourself first**

It's true what they say on airlines about putting your own oxygen mask on before helping other people. When someone you love dies you won't be the only one affected by grief, but your recovery has to be priority for you. This doesn't mean you can't support your friends or family. But remember the concept of detachment, and follow your own path to healing. Other people may heal at a different speed to you, either more slowly or more quickly. In an unexpected way, my mum seemed to take longer to process my husband's death than I did, perhaps because it brought up fears around my dad's mortality. Every person's grief is different, depending on their past and coping mechanisms. Ask yourself every day what you need and honour your unique route to recovery. Only then can you find the strength to help people who are behind you.

SIXTEEN

What's the Soul-ution?
Past Lives and Old Triggers

Last year at an Australia Day barbecue, I met a mother whose daughter had died of an eating disorder 22 years earlier. Her daughter, who was a medical student, had convinced a doctor to give her a prescription for beta-blockers, after she realised that her heart rate was speeding up due to her lack of nourishment. The doctor didn't realise that she was starving herself, so the medication should never have been prescribed to someone in her condition. After an autopsy, her parents learnt that she'd taken a handful of pills at once, which stopped her heart completely.

After hearing the family's story which they shared with me so generously, I opened up about my own turbulent relationship with food. Interestingly, the parents said they saw a lot of similarities in our experiences and the way I talked about my fear of eating. That mother went on to train as a therapist working at a school where she helps teenagers cope with coming-of-age challenges, including self-esteem and eating issues. When I finished telling my story, she asked a question that I've asked myself a thousand times over the years: What do you think caused your eating disorder in the first place?

In the past, therapists, friends and Dr. Google have offered many different theories on the reason: my perfectionist mentality, my toxic relationship with my first boyfriend, the loneliness of university and my father's cancer. I'm sure all of these factors had an impact but, if I'm honest, none of those reasons have ever really resonated with me. None of the reasons have fully explained why, halfway through my adolescence, I began to feel such utter terror at the thought of eating that I would rather risk my life than do so.

Years of therapy and self-exploration didn't give me an answer, although I was grateful they gave me the tools to heal and self-manage my eating demons. I had accepted that I would probably never discover why I'd become trapped in that mindset—until a meeting with my spiritual healer uncovered the answer in a past that I didn't know existed.

I had gone to see Yvonne, as I always do when I come back to England for a visit. My husband and I were about to go backpacking across South America and then home to start trying for a baby, so I wanted to make sure my body was healthy, nurtured, strong and able to start a family. Our session started as normal with an hour of talking, before moving onto body work, aura healing and colour acupuncture.

We began by talking about my work, our plans to travel and our hopes for starting a family. Over the years, Yvonne has done a lot of work to release trauma from my body, so that my period could return after its absence. At this time, my period was still irregular and I suspected that, with the stress of travel and change that lay ahead of us, it might disappear completely—not ideal when we wanted to conceive in the future.

That's when Yvonne told me a story about my past. More to the point, she channelled a story that was shown to her. She was shown an image of a young girl playing with a young boy next to a river. They were in love but the girl's parents had promised her to another man who was older, richer and more suitable. The girl was due to get married after her menstrual cycle started, as that confirmed she was a woman. But before the wedding could take place, shortly after her seventeenth birthday, the girl drank contaminated water from the river and died. The little girl in the vision was me. The little boy was my husband. The scene was from our past life together.

'I'm being shown this now so you can understand, at last, your relationship with food,' said Yvonne. 'It's a soul fear, because you were poisoned.' This was like someone handing me a missing chapter from my story—an entire missing book from my life's library. My eating disorder made sense to me in an instant.

My body was remembering my past life on a cellular level. That's why I felt so frightened about trying any new food that could harm me and, during my eating disorder, only ate from a short list of 'safe' foods that I had to prepare myself, so I knew exactly what went into them. It also explained why my eating disorder began when I was seventeen because I associated becoming a woman with danger. 'You want to be a sexy, voluptuous woman; but you're frightened you're going to put something into your body which will hurt you and take you away from the man you love,' explained Yvonne.

When I was writing this chapter I remembered, for the first time, another illogical fear and obsessive behaviour from my childhood. When I was about seven years old, I saw a member of my family buying sanitary products. When I asked what they were, she gave me a brief explanation about why women need them. Over the next year I became obsessed with checking my urine for blood—at the age of seven. I'd peer into the toilet, terrified that I'd see a red droplet in the water. Once, in the middle of the night, I woke up my dad in a panic, because I thought I'd seen a red tinge in the fluid. I wonder if, in my past life, I felt the same fear when I first got my period, knowing I was about to lose my freedom, the boy I loved—and later my life.

☐ SHE'S BEHIND YOU

This story and the idea of having multiple lives will not resonate with everyone who reads it. If I hadn't experienced the 'aha' moment myself, I might well be sceptical. Until then, I didn't really have an opinion when it came to past lives or reincarnation. But as soon as I heard the story, it resonated deeply inside me and I knew it was the answer to a decade of unexplained issues.

This isn't the only way my past life has affected me. When I became pregnant, all of a sudden I developed an intense fear of water. My husband and I live a few minutes from the ocean and spend every weekend surfing, swimming or snorkelling. It is my happy place! But one Sunday, as I waded into the ocean, fear washed over me. It was so shocking, so consuming, that I froze knee-deep in the water.

To my astonishment, I started sobbing. When I looked back at my husband standing on the shore, I sobbed harder. At the point where I would usually have dived joyfully into the ocean, I felt stricken with sadness and a feeling I identified as grief. I heard myself saying, 'I don't want to do it. I don't want to do it.' I stood there crying, with my arms wrapped around my body, until I realised I couldn't go in further and turned back to the shore, shaking.

The next night I Skyped my spiritual healer for an emergency session. What was wrong with me? And how could I move past it? The ocean is a big part of our lives and I had always dreamt of it being part of my daughter's life too. Where was this irrational fear coming from and how could I overcome it?

During our session, Yvonne was shown an extra layer of my story. When I drank water from the river, I knew that it was contaminated, I knew it was probably going to kill me and yet I drank it anyway, because I didn't see any other way out of my arranged marriage. As I stood in the water in my current life, this old memory emerged, along with the sentence that I had spoken at the time ('I don't want to do it') and the deep grief that I'd felt at leaving the boy I loved behind.

Depending on your belief system, you may or may not believe in reincarnation. However for me, hearing about my past was pivotal in helping me to heal in the present.

To overcome my fear of water I went to a calm, clear bay and was patient with myself as I tiptoed into the still water. When I felt fear in my stomach—my sacral chakra—I imagined blasting it with orange light and asked the area of my body tainted with fear from my past to let it go.

Today, whenever I feel overwhelming anxiety about eating a new food or wading into deep water, I ask myself: 'Is this a real fear or an old memory?' I no longer feel terror when other people cook for me, even if I don't know the meal's ingredients. I can run down the beach and throw myself into the water, laughing. I found the soul-ution to my problems at last.

☐ LEARNING TO LOVE YOUR SELVES

Whether or not you believe in rebirth, all of our lives are made up of episodes. I personally feel like I've already lived a dozen lives in one, as I look back on my 32 years and the different periods that define them. I could line up my former 'selves' like an evolutionary diagram from monkey to man. My own 'March of Progress' would show my different selves in their different habitats: a classroom, a bathroom, a hospital, a nightclub, a magazine office and a forest.

We can all remember some stages of our lives with perfect clarity, but it's the moments of our lives that we've forgotten that could hold vital clues to our happiness.

⌒ Do you have an illogical fear you can't fathom?
⌒ Do you have a toxic habit that started without reason?
⌒ Do you have an attraction to certain types of people who aren't good for you?

○ Does a certain place, face, smell, taste or tone of voice stir up strong feelings inside you?
○ Have you felt scared or anxious all of your life—but have no idea why?

If you can't pinpoint when or why a cycle of behaviour started, if you can't uncover the origin of a fear or find logic in an illogical way of thinking, the answer may not be in your memories. It might be in a period of your life—or a past life—that you've forgotten or chosen to block from your memory for a reason.

Shortly before the magazine I edited closed, I got the opportunity to visit a health retreat in the Hunter Valley to write about their new holistic wellbeing program. As part of the schedule, I was booked in for a session with their in-house hypnotherapist. Until this point, I had thought hypnotherapy was for quitting smoking or getting over a fear of flying, but I went along with it because it was research for my magazine article. I didn't realise their hypnotherapist specialised in inner child exploration. I didn't expect to end up lying on her couch, sobbing with sadness and relief.

If you haven't experienced hypnotherapy, it's not like you see in movies. It's really more akin to a meditative state, with the help of the hypnotherapist guiding you into a deep sense of relaxation. As I lay on my back on the couch, Sonja asked me an unexpected question: 'What is your earliest memory of feeling sad?' Instead of overthinking the answer, an image came into my head. I was seven years old, standing in the hallway of my old gymnastics studio and I was crying.

Sonja told me to approach myself. When I asked the little girl (me!) what was wrong, she looked up with big, wet eyes and said, 'I have to quit, because I'm not good enough anymore.' More than two decades into the future, as I lay on the hypnotherapist's couch, I felt my heart break. 'All I wanted to do was play,' said the little girl, 'But I'm not good enough, so I have to stop.'

I found myself sobbing along with my seven-year-old self. I felt so incredibly sad for her, standing there alone. My inner child was—is—perfect. She had energy and joy. She should never have stopped playing. Yet I'd judged her and starved her, criticised her and constrained her. More than anything, I hadn't comforted her when she needed me the most.

As our session drew to a close, Sonja told me to take the little girl's hand. I told her I was sorry I'd left her. I told her I was sorry that I hadn't comforted her. I told her I was sorry she'd waited so long for me. I told her I'd never leave her alone again. When I finished the session, I took the little girl 'with' me, imagining her glowing silhouette merging into my adult body. It was one of the most incredible healing moments I've ever experienced.

My 'homework' after the session was to incorporate playtime into my life, whether it was doing cartwheels on the beach or baking sweet, sticky cakes on the weekend, and dedicate the activity to my inner child. Today, when I go out running—a hobby that I used to take far too seriously—I skip, jump and leap to touch the lowest branches on trees overhead. A few after my hypnotherapy session, and I decided to join an adult gymnastics class once a week.

My inner critic worried I wouldn't be good enough, but I let my inner child make the call.

At certain points in our lives, we block out memories for different reasons. It might be because you were too young (according to research, few adults can remember anything before the age of three and a half[1]) or because you've never considered that a particular incident was significant.

Can you think about an early time in your life when you felt sad, anxious, disappointed, betrayed or felt like a dream was taken away from you?

A lot can be learnt from visiting our past temporarily, especially if you're suffering from an illogical anxiety, worry or phobia and have no idea what is causing it. Although I don't believe in living in the past, it can pay to recollect (re-collect) memories that you've left behind, whether you read back on an old journal, reminisce with a trusted family member or engage in the help of a professional.

During meditation, I imagine that I'm 're-collecting' memories that are strewn around me, like pieces of paper torn from a magazine. In my mind, I see myself picking one of the pieces of paper off the ground. Sometimes it's a photograph of myself at a certain age and sometimes the clue is more subtle—the silhouette of a face, the garden of a house, the fabric of a sofa. I sit with this image and see what feelings it evokes and what I can learn from them.

I interviewed the actress Drew Barrymore after the release of her memoir Wildflower, a collection of essays about her turbulent early years and path to happiness. She told me she found writing the book incredibly therapeutic because, 'I was looking in the rear mirror while being more in the present than I've ever been.' I love that description of recollection—the idea that you can peer back into your past, while still keeping two hands on the steering wheel of your present.

When I was writing this chapter, my mum told me about a ritual our old Catholic priest used to do every evening. Father Adrien would say a prayer for his father who had fought in World War Two, sending him the courage and bravery he needed in the trenches. It didn't matter that the war had ended over fifty years before, or that his father had died a lifetime later in a nursing home. He believed it was still important to send daily love and support to his father during the toughest challenge of his life, even though it was far behind him.

It's never too late to support your younger self, to listen to your needs and offer yourself comfort. You can't step into a time machine but you can send your energy back to a time and a place where you needed it the most. In the evening after I have a shower, I sometimes stand in front of the mirror, place my palms over my womb and close my eyes. I think of the versions of myself that I've been—both in this life and in past lives—and the versions of myself that I may become in the future. I send love, courage, happiness and hope to all these versions of me. And for a moment, I gather them into my mind together.

If I hadn't recollected my inner child, I wouldn't have as much playfulness or compassion in my life. Is your inner child waiting somewhere for you?

☐ HOW TO FIND YOUR INNER CHILD

☐ Sit or lie in a place where you feel safe.

☐ Breathe in for four seconds, hold for four seconds, breathe out for four seconds. Repeat this until you feel your shoulders relaxing. Focus on the muscles that frame your eye sockets. Relax them.

☐ Ask yourself:

When was the first time in my life I remember feeling scared?

When was the first time in my life I remember feeling anxious?

When was the first time in my life I remember feeling ashamed?

☐ Let an image of your younger self rise into your mind; where are you, what are you doing and, most importantly, how are you feeling?

☐ Approach your inner child and take her hand. Tell yourself, 'I'm sorry that I have left you alone. I'm sorry that I didn't come back for your sooner. I'm sorry that I haven't comforted you earlier. But I'm here for you now. I will take care of you.'

☐ At this point, I like to imagine absorbing my inner child into my body, but you might prefer to take their hand and let them walk beside you.

☐ Every day for the next two weeks, do something to make your inner child smile: take a bubble bath, read a book, lie on the grass or do a creative activity.

☐ After the two weeks is over, continue to carry your inner child with you and consider it an honour to nourish and nurture her. Show her the moon, point out the stars, draw her attention to a rainbow. If the old fear, anxiety or shame surfaces again, hold her close and tell her, 'I hear you. I am here.'

SEVENTEEN

Is It Time to Let Yourself Off the Naughty Step?

Recently, I spoke to a friend who has been struggling after a break-up. The guy she was dating for over a year ended their relationship in the most unbelievable manner, suddenly cutting her out of his life, not returning her phone calls or replying to her emails. He simply disappeared one day (she knows he is alive and well, as she can see that he's active on social media).

Unsurprisingly, the break-up hit her hard. She blamed herself and, since the split, has analysed everything that she did and said in the lead-up to the end, looking for clues and blaming herself for not being a 'better' girlfriend. I was beginning to get very worried as I watched her mentally spiral downwards, especially as she has a history of self-harm and eating disorders.

But when I phoned her yesterday, I could tell instantly that she sounded different—lighter, brighter, and altogether more peaceful. 'I decided it was time to let myself off the naughty step,' she said. 'I can't keep punishing myself for what I did or didn't do differently.'

What an amazing analogy! After the end of the relationship, she had shouldered all of the blame and, in doing so, emotionally relegated herself to a grey square, isolated, ashamed, constrained and lonely. The moment she decided to take herself 'off the naughty step' she immediately felt freer. 'I realised that every day I was beating myself up, I was damaging myself more,' she said. 'I can't change his mind about our relationship—and nor do I want to—but I can change my mind about myself.'

⊙ How many people have placed themselves on a naughty step in the past?

⊙ Perhaps you're mentally trapped there right now?

When we experience a loss, betrayal, trauma, tragedy or disappointment, when our lives don't go exactly the way we hoped or expected, how many of us point the finger of blame at ourselves? We criticise ourselves, punish ourselves, reprimand ourselves and chastise ourselves, long after the sadness, anger or anxiety from that particular incident has passed.

⊙ Are you quick to forgive other people, but slow to forgive yourself?

⊙ Do you shoulder 100 percent of the blame and believe you're 100 percent at fault for any unfortunate situation or conflict?

We extend our misery by disciplining ourselves. How many of us become isolated and reclusive after a tough patch, not answering phone calls and turning down all social invitations? This is giving yourself a 'timeout' on your life! How many people have banned themselves from dating for a certain period after a difficult break-up; or decided to stick with a job they hate, until another problem in their life has 'settled down'? These are all forms of self-punishment—you're confining yourself to a naughty step of your own making. And by doing so, you're extending your own pain and suffering.

When someone we love lets us down, whether it's an ex-partner, a best friend or a parent, forgiving them can sometimes be easy (because we love them!) but forgiving ourselves can be much harder. It's also a lot more exhausting because, unlike an ex-boyfriend you can unfollow on Facebook, the person you feel let you down stares back in the mirror every morning.

I'm not saying you should let yourself off the hook entirely. Some people believe that guilt is not a wasted emotion—it alerts us to actions that don't fit within our value system and helps us to maintain relationships by learning from past interactions and uncomfortable circumstances. But once you've acknowledged the lesson, once you've realised you won't act that way again now that you're older and more experienced, clinging to that guilt is a form self-sabotage that stops you from reaching your potential.

There are still memories in my head that are unsettling to poke at. My dad rushing out of the front door shouting, 'All I ever wanted was a happy family!' My sister feeling like she'd lost me. My mum praying that she'd die in place of my husband. An argument I had with him a week before he died, because I was angry he'd ordered a cocktail when he wasn't meant to be drinking. One cocktail! Why couldn't I have let him enjoy it?

Whenever I think of these moments, I walk myself to the naughty step—a place of shame, blame and constriction. How can you move forward, when you can't take a single step in any direction? What kind of life can you lead from there?

☐ THE STIGMA OF THE DIFFICULT CHILD

The power of forgiveness is a huge topic. I'm still a work in process, as I continue to sieve through the memories in my mental archive and stumble upon guilt which I didn't know existed. In Chinese medicine, guilt is thought to block your qi (the energetic flow around your body). According to research, unresolved guilt can interfere with cognitive function and concentration. New research shows differences in the brains of kids who show excessively guilty behaviour, which may put them at risk for a host of mood disorders as adults.[1]

Guilt domination, according to Louise Hay, can manifest as pain in the middle of your back, symbolic of the fact you're carrying weight from your past. A study from Princeton found there could be truth in the metaphor 'weighed down by guilt.' During the research, participants were asked to carry bags of groceries up some stairs. They were then asked to recall a time when they acted unethically and repeat the task. They reported finding it harder and feeling like their bodies were heavier when they were feeling guilty.[1] Unlike sadness or anger which, as emotions go, are easy to identify, guilt may be holding you back, emotionally or physically, without you even realising it.

Shortly after my 32nd birthday, I realised that I was still carrying the stigma of being a difficult teenager, when symptoms began to show up in my relationship—nearly two decades after I first entered adolescence. I couldn't understand why, in my current very contented relationship, I was so anxious about offering an opinion that differed from his.

Whether it was about what we should do at the weekend, how long we should spend backpacking across South America or how many guests to invite to our wedding, I would say 'whatever you think'—even when my gut feeling said it wasn't the right choice for me. Then my agreeability came back to bite me. Halfway across Bolivia and only a month before our wedding, I realised we were throwing a house party for 150 people.

'Why didn't you tell me you were worried about it?' my husband asked every time, as I inevitably had a meltdown when it was too late to change anything. It was a good question! When it comes to my work, I have no problem voicing my opinion. I know my husband is a good listener and would always respect my opinion, but I still felt anxious and guilty at the thought of putting my opinion forward.

After one particular incident, which involved me crying by the side of the road on the way up a mountain, I decided to sit down and meditate on the issue. I imagined my mind was a white projector screen and I waited for the answer to appear across the canvas. It didn't take long for four words to fight their way through: Don't be difficult. Again. I could hear the voice of my parents in my head, 'Amy has always been the difficult one.' I saw a journal entry I wrote as a teenager: 'Every argument in this house is all my fault.' I remembered my dad throwing a plate of toast at the wall as he begged me to eat and, years later, my parents paying for a wedding that had to be organised in three weeks, for a marriage that lasted the same length of time.

The words spun in my head: Don't be difficult Amy. Don't be difficult. Again.

My guilt from the past was affecting the flow of my relationship, even though those past events had nothing to do with our connection. I was scared that, if I disagreed with my husband even once, he would uncover my deep dark secret—that I'm a difficult person. He would look at me in the way my parents had looked at me in the past; he would decide that I was too much of a hassle, that I was too much work to manage.

It was an illogical fear, because I know for a fact it annoys him that I refuse to ever make a decision, so it's always left up to him. But guilt doesn't deal in logic, which is why it's so dangerous. Guilt, by its nature, distorts your vision of yourself and of the people around you. It makes you project the feelings you have about yourself onto the people who love you.

☐ THE ENEMY WITHIN

In my experience, guilt is cumulative. If you don't process it, it increases over time because you feel like the opportunity has passed to address it or make amends for it. But it's never too late to say sorry; it's never too late to discuss it; and it's never too late to let the guilt go that you've been carrying for a lifetime. I listen to a lot of guided meditation tracks on forgiveness (Gabrielle Bernstein has great ones in her books). During my journalling workshops, I often ask participants to write a letter of forgiveness directed at the source of their emotions (download 'forgiveness letter templates' online, if you need help getting started). As part of my journey, I've had to forgive myself for not being able to forgive myself faster too.

My psychotherapist once told me that you have to deal with guilt as you'd deal with a hangover: 'Sit in a dark room in silence, rest and drink lots of water.' It can be uncomfortable to sit with your feelings on guilt but, when you understand where they're coming from, you can address them and stop them affecting your new relationships and connections.

Today, when my husband asks for my opinion I make an effort to respond mindfully, before automatically agreeing with him. I still go along with him sometimes, even if it's not my first choice, but the compromise comes from a place of love rather than a place of fear. And if I do change my mind, I try to tell him sooner rather than later.

As humans, our capacity to forgive is incredible, not only ourselves but also other people. During my journey back to forgiveness, I interviewed Katy Hutchison, an American mother of twin sons. Katy's husband Bill was beaten to death after going to their neighbour's house to check on a disturbance, leaving her widowed with their four-year-old twins. After the killer was sentenced, Katy went to visit him in prison. 'The boy in front of me sobbing for forgiveness didn't look like a murderer,' she said. 'He looked broken and lost . . . I just wanted the pain to end, for both of us. As he sobbed, it was all I could do not to hold him. Second to the day I gave birth, it was probably the most human moment of my life.'

You don't have to forgive yourself or the people that you feel have wronged you. You can continue to carry that extra weight for the rest of your life, but it will exacerbate your suffering. Resisting forgiveness drains energy, resisting forgiveness creates roughness. Is it time you smoothed over your relationship with yourself?

You did the best you could
WITH THE TOOLS YOU HAD AT THE TIME

Write out the above heading and stick it on your bathroom mirror; carry it around in your wallet, put in under your pillow, or leave it anywhere you are likely to see it in your most guilt-stricken moment. I first heard this sentence from my life coach, when I was talking about my actions after I was widowed. It felt like a light had been switched on beneath my eyes. I knew that she was right.

You might look back on your life now and say to yourself: 'How could I have done that?' You were probably doing the best you could with the tools you had at that time, at that age, with the life experiences you had in that moment. You can't regret or feel shame around your actions, when you did the best that you could.

EIGHTEEN

Don't Let the Worst Day of Your Life Be Your Greatest Achievement

I'll always remember a conversation I had with my mum shortly after my husband died. 'To me you're done,' she said. 'If you do nothing else with your life this is enough for me.' She had seen me nurse a man to his death; she'd watched me get married and, three weeks later, walk down a church aisle behind a coffin. After all that I didn't need to achieve anything else in her eyes. I had nothing left to prove, or to do.

At the time, I agreed with her sentiment. I believed that I was placed on this earth for one purpose: to be an 'apprentice' carer during my dad's cancer, so that I would have the skills I needed to ease my husband's passing. At the age of 21, I'd already conquered my life's mission. I'd stepped up, I'd been strong and I'd stood beside him until his final breath. Tick, done, accomplished!

Over the next few years, although I was still ambitious when it came to my career, I knew that anything I achieved in the future would come second to my most significant accomplishment. On a good day, this made me feel proud; but on a bad day, it made me self-destructive. I got into relationships with men who I didn't like, let alone love, because I figured that my greatest love—the one—had already happened. I told my best friend that I would never have a baby because, 'I've already served my time taking care of someone.' At times I was selfish, thoughtless and angry, directing it at my friends and my family. I felt like I had the ultimate get-out clause to do whatever I liked— or not do anything at all—because I already had so many 'selfless' credits in the bank.

In a sense, grief made me conceited—and selfish. My sister once told me that I manipulated our parents with my drama. I played on it. I milked it. I would say, repeatedly, that I didn't want to be defined as a widow, but I really did. The worst day of my life was my greatest achievement. What accomplishment could make my family prouder or make society think more of me than that?

○ Do your past struggles make you feel special?
○ Do you wonder who you'd be without them?
○ Is the worst day of your life your greatest achievement?

This isn't a bad way to feel about yourself. In fact, you could say this entire book is about feeling proud of your toughest moments. We live in a world where survivors are held in high regard, as they should be. In movies, the female lead has to face hardship before she can find her happy ending.

On television talent shows, the most popular singers are the ones with the toughest sob story.

The problem arises when you use the past as an excuse to not to reach your full potential; when you accept it as your unique selling point, when you write off the rest of your life because you're already a survivor—and what could put you in a more powerful position?

The British actress Jennifer Saunders, who wrote an auto-biography about her battle with breast cancer, has talked about the social status that having cancer can give you. When asked if she believed some people keep wearing cancer like a badge of honour she responded, 'Forever— because it's the best job you don't have to work for. You suddenly get so much attention.'

Identifying as a survivor can also protect you, because how can you be mean to someone who has been through so much? In his book Modern Yoga, Australian yoga teacher Duncan Peak, the founder of Power Living, talks about the reasons people choose to identify themselves as a victim, saying: 'They use their stories of the past—of how they were a victim, the world was against them or they were hard done by—to manipulate a situation or to get the result of people feeling sorry for them or not challenging them.'

Here's the truth – a past trauma can be a powerful weapon.

When I was 24 and trying to break into the magazine industry, an editor only agreed to meet me for an interview, because she'd recognised my name from an article I'd written about being widowed. In a pile of résumés, it had made me stand out. She offered me an (unpaid) internship and the only reason I could afford to undertake it was because, for the first few years after losing my husband, I got a Widow's Pension from the Irish government until I began another relationship.

The truth is that, although I wouldn't wish it on anybody, being a widow opened doors for me. For a long time, it was my unique selling point and made people think I was a good person. But every time someone told me I was 'inspirational' for 'what you've been through' I couldn't shake a niggling feeling—wouldn't it be better if my greatest achievement was something a little more positive?

I kept coming back to the words of my mother: 'To me you're done. If you do nothing else with your life, this is enough for me.' I know she meant it as the ultimate compliment but, as a woman in her twenties, had I really hit my peak on the day they lowered my husband's lifeless body into the earth?

Of all the interviews I've conducted over the years, I've always been inspired by people who managed to use their toughest times as triggers. They don't try to find 'closure' (a word that I've never related to) but instead use the worst moment of their lives as step one on a path leading to an achievement that made them shine more brightly.

There are so many incredible people I've had the pleasure of interviewing over the years. My friend Scott Maggs, creator of the skin cancer awareness organisation, Beard Season, was inspired by the loss of his best friend Wes, who died of malignant melanoma like my husband. Ingrid Newkirk, president of animal rights group PETA, was taken by her mother to a leper colony when she was a child, so

A writing exercise:

COMPLETE EACH PARAGRAPH . . .

I am . . .

I used to be . . .

I want to be . . .

she could learn about suffering. Social entrepreneur Jules Allen has fostered 32 children in the past two decades. Her journey as a foster mother began when she was just 22, working as a social worker after escaping with her two-year-old son from an abusive relationship.

Whenever I asked such people about their greatest achievements, they didn't focus on the worst thing that had ever happened to them, although they admitted it was a pivotal part of their journey. Instead they talked about what came afterwards. They had taken that life experience and not let it become static, instead allowing it to evolve, emerge and expand.

The reality is that turning your pain into purpose isn't always easy.

After I decided I could no longer cling to the identity of being a widow, for a brief period I was convinced that I should quit journalism and become a nurse, until I realised that caring for one terminal man doesn't give you the education to make it a vocation. I also applied to work at a hospice for cancer patients, but was politely rejected because they felt I needed to focus on my own healing.

I was desperate to find a 'higher purpose' for what had happened to me, but I was thinking too lineally. Although starting your own not-for-profit or caring for sick children is admirable, it's not for everybody. So what lasting skills had my early life given me and how could I package them up and re-gift them?

○ You might be in this place right now.
○ You've survived.

- You're still standing.
- You're no longer numb.
- You're no longer angry.
- You want to move forward.

So . . . what's next?

If you're anything like me, you spend your life looking for signs. I'd be asked to speak at a skin cancer event and think, 'This will be it. I'll soon be the new face of skin cancer awareness.' (I wasn't.) I'd post a photo on my Instagram feed of my first husband, with a deep and moving caption, then expect it to go viral. (It didn't.) I scanned the horizon constantly for my new life purpose, desperately looking for meaning in my former misery.

I never did find my purpose—but my purpose found me.

You are reading it—the product of a decade of interviews, driven by my desire to understand resilience, happiness, hope and recovery. Funnily enough, while I was busy searching for my purpose, I was quietly and subtly living it; by going to work every day, phoning people and filing articles. Even as a junior journalist, fresh out of university, I was able to put myself in other people's shoes because of my early challenges. I found that people opened up with me. I could imagine what they'd been though and find the words to describe it.

Because of my time spent in 'Chemo Club' with my dad, I wasn't afraid of tackling heavy subjects with people of all ages and backgrounds. I felt no fear or awkwardness around discussing death, asking a dying man about his feelings on euthanasia or asking a widow if she ever thought about suicide after the death of her husband.

Because of my years in therapy, I knew how to explain tools like the Emotional Freedom Technique, meditation and mindfulness, long before they became trendy and common knowledge. When writing articles, I had a little black book of mental health professionals that I could call on to offer an expert opinion and I knew how to explain their jargon in layman's terms—because I'd been a patient myself.

Without all of my early challenges, I wouldn't be half the journalist I am. On my computer, I have a folder containing emails and screen grabs of text messages that people have sent to me after I interviewed them saying 'thank you.' One of my most treasured is from a famous Australian businessman who I spoke to about the death of his father. 'What a magical job you've done capturing my feelings perfectly,' it says. 'I'm in tears. You've helped me to process my pain.'

I have a lot to thank these people for. Every person that I've interviewed, every conversation I've had and connection I've made has also helped me to digest my own past and heal my own wounds.

A stranger once wrote under one of my online articles, 'For god's sake, will she ever stop writing about her dead husband?' To be honest, probably not! But it's not all that I will do. Although walking my husband from this earth was a great honour, if you asked me about my greatest achievement it wouldn't be at the top of my list, or even in the top five.

Today, my greatest achievement is a lot less extraordinary than my past experiences. My greatest achievement is contentment and the ease in which I can now live. On an average day, I wake up and squeeze my husband, go to the same cafe, order the same pot of chai tea, sit in the same seat and write with a smile on my face. That doesn't mean I'm 'cured.' I practise all the techniques that I talk about in this book every day and I still face constant challenges. (We all do!) But even on tough days, I can keep gliding onwards. I can look back on my past while still facing forwards.

As I wrote this final chapter, sitting cross-legged in a coffee shop, an elderly woman approached me. 'I just have to say, I've been watching you for a while,' she said. 'You look so peaceful and contented. Your baby is very lucky to be around that.' An old echo in my head said, 'Imagine if she knew what you've been through! Tell her!' But I no longer feel like I need to use my past to make an impression. Instead, I thanked her and accepted the compliment, not for the girl that I once was, but for the woman that I am today.

We all have the capacity to evolve and grow with every challenge, and the challenges will keep coming. Your worst days might be behind you or you could still have some ahead. When you have faith in your abilities to recover—joyfully—the threat of future struggles can't steal your power anymore. You know that challenges can make you even more limitless than before.

I can't tell you exactly where to go from here, or how to turn your own pain into a new purpose, but I hope that you now have hope. The hope that you are not broken, damaged or beyond repair. The hope that there's always tomorrow. The realisation that your greatest achievement—which could be contentment—can always be ahead of you, not matter what's behind you.

I hope that, every day, I continue to meet amazing people who've survived amazing experiences. One day perhaps I'll have the honour of hearing about your story.

Every person, every problem, every incredible story of hope and recovery reminds me that . . . the world is a nice place.

If you want it to be.

EPILOGUE

All the Lessons Led to This

There will be moments in your life when all your challenges make sense; when all your coping mechanisms, your
lessons and the insights you've discovered about yourself
come together, bond together and make you feel invincible.
When you realise the immense power you hold inside yourself; when you realise this is what you've been training for.

For me, this moment came at the birth of my baby
daughter.

In the final weeks leading up to her arrival, knowing
I'd prefer her birth to be as natural as possible, I leant on
every strategy, every coping mechanism and every ounce
of self-belief that I'd developed during my journey.

In the early stages of labour, when my contractions were
far apart, I focused on distraction and relaxation, walking
on the beach, writing, baking, meditating and creating. As
my contractions grew closer, I focused on movement, doing
yoga in the sunshine and dancing with my eyes closed,

feeling the flow of energy through my body. To ground myself when the surges intensified, I imagined standing in a forest with my palms on a smooth, cool tree trunk.

I used the mantra: I am safe, I am whole, I choose peace.

I had made it clear to our midwives that, although I wanted a natural birth, if my baby was in any danger my plans should go out the window. But as I laboured, I knew from the beginning that it would be okay. I had signed a soul contract to experience this journey whatever the outcome.

I felt the power within me of all the younger versions of myself—the dangerously premature baby, the child with obsessive-compulsive tendencies, the teenager with an eating disorder and the 23-year-old widow. I felt all my younger selves join hands and combine lessons, knowing that the unimaginable is survivable and that even the most painful moments are impermanent and will pass.

At times I became introverted, entering my own world of mantras and visions. At other moments, I roared like a lion, releasing the force of the energy inside my body. In the Indian tradition, there is the belief that the toughest point of labour—the transition—is a rite of passage which transforms you from maiden to mother. When women get through this stage they are allowed to make a wish, which I did. I love this concept—the belief that, after the most painful experience in your life, you can get anything your heart desires.

As I write this, our little girl is strapped to my chest in a sling. We called her Pasha, inspired by Pachamama or Mother Earth and our hope that she is a passionate spirit. She came into this world crying, shocked by a pool of cool water, but soon she was peaceful and content again. Now 11 months old, she lives utterly in the moment, expressing fear or discomfort unashamedly, but then letting it go completely, as soon as that moment is behind her.

I know that, over the coming years, our daughter will face her own unique challenges and also challenge us as her parents. But I can't wish away any part of her journey. All my lessons led me to her. And her lessons will lead her to the limitless life she was born to lead.

I hope to help her flow through them, just as I hope this book has helped you too.

References

☐ **INTRODUCTION**

1. Adverse childhood experiences in Minnesota, 2011 Minnesota Behavioral Risk Factor Surveillance System, accessed 26 September 2017. www.health.state.mn.us/divs/chs/brfss/ACE_Executive-Summary.pdf

☐ **CHAPTER 1**

2. Smart and Illicit: Who Becomes an Entrepreneur and Do They Earn More? Ross Levine and Yona Rubinstein, September 13 2015, the Quarterly Journal of Economic, accessed 26 September 2017. https://funginstitute.berkeley.edu/wp-content/uploads/2015/09/smart_and_illicit_13sep2015.pdf
3. A mixed blessing? Dual mediating mechanisms in the relationship between dopamine transporter gene DAT1 and leadership role occupancy, Wen-dong Li et al, October 2015, The Leadership Quarterly, accessed 26 September 2017. www.sciencedirect.com.

☐ **CHAPTER 4**

4. Family rituals; what are they? Raising Children Network, August 5 2015, Raisingchildren.net.au. accessed 26 September

2017. http://raisingchildren.net.au/articles/rituals_and_how_
they_work.html

☐ CHAPTER 6

5. Addicted To Chaos: The Journey From Extreme To Serene, Doctor Keith Lee, 2007, Transformational Life Coaching & Consulting
6. Planning 'Worry Time' May Help Ease Anxiety, Joe Brownstein, July 26 2011, LiveScience, accessed 26 September 2017. https:// www.livescience.com/15233-planning-worry-time-ease-anxiety. html
7. A Better Path to High Performance, Erin O'Donnell, May-June 2014, Harvard Magazine, accessed 26 September 2017. http:// harvardmagazine. com/2014/05/a-better-path-to-high-performance

☐ CHAPTER 7

8. Make More Art: The Health Benefits of Creativity, James Clear, December 23 2015, The Huffington Post, accessed 26 September 2017. http://www.huffingtonpost.com/james-clear/make-more-art-the-health-benefits-of-creativity_b_8868802.html
9. Flow, the secret to happiness, Mihaly Csikszentmihalyi, TED talks, accessed 26 September 2017. https://www.ted.com/talks/ mihaly_csikszentmihalyi_on_flow/transcript?language=en

☐ CHAPTER 8

10. Sibling configurations, educational aspiration and attainment, Feifei Bu, November 2014, EconPapers, accessed 26 September 2017. http://econpapers.repec.org/paper/eseiserwp/2014-11. htm
11. The relationships between perfectionism, pathological worry and generalised anxiety disorder, Handley et al. licensee BioMed Central Ltd. 2014, BMC Psychiatry, accessed 26 September 2017. https://bmcpsychiatry.biomedcentral.com/art-icles/10.1186/1471-244X-14-98
12. Perfectionism Can Kill Women's Self Esteem And Sex Life: Why Sexual Arousal Isn't As Chemical As You Think, Ali Venosa,

March 2016, Medical Daily, accessed 26 September 2017. http://
www.medicaldaily.com/perfectionism-female-sexual-dysfunc-
tion-low-self-esteem-380131

13. Are you suffering from Brownout? Rhymer Rigby, September 15
2015, The Telegraph, accessed 26 September 2017. http://www.
telegraph.co.uk/men/the-filter/11866571/Are-you-suffering-
from-brownout.html

14. Redundancy can get you a payrise, survey reveals, March 14
2012, WorkPlace Info, accessed 26 September 2017. http://www.
workplaceinfo.com.au/termination/redundancy/redundancy-
can-get-you-a-pay-rise-survey-reveals

☐ CHAPTER 12

15. Forget siestas, 'green micro-breaks' could boost work productivity, Kate Lee et al, May 28 2015, The Conversation, accessed 26
September 2017. http://theconversation.com/forget-siestas-
green-micro-breaks-could-boost-work-productivity-42356

16. The Road to Resilience, American Psychological Association,
accessed 26 September 2017. http://www.apa.org/helpcenter/
road-resilience.aspx

☐ CHAPTER 13

17. Survey: Entrepreneurs Are Happiest People On Planet, Elaine
Pofeldt, March 5 2014, Forbes, accessed 26 September 2017.
https://www.forbes.com/sites/elainepofeldt/2014/03/05/sur-
vey-entrepreneurs-are-happier-than-employees/#5854482262d9

18. My experience with resilience, Sir Richard Branson, October 28
2016, Virgin, accessed 26 September 2016. https://www.virgin.
com/richard-branson/my-experience-resilience

☐ CHAPTER 15

19. Family Characteristics and Transitions, Australia, 2012-13, Australian Bureau of Statistics, accessed 26 September 2017. http://
www.abs.gov.au/ausstats/abs@.nsf/mf/4442.0

20. Maternal separation stresses the baby, research finds, Elsevier,
November 2, 2011, Science Daily, accessed 26 September 2017.

https://www.sciencedaily.com/releases/2011/11/111102124955.htm

☐ CHAPTER 16

21. Childhood memories; why are they so difficult to recall? Jeanne Shinsky, July 18 2016, The Independent, accessed 26 September 2017. http://www.independent.co.uk/life-style/health-and-families/childhood-memories-research-early-development-recollection--culture-a7142361.html

☐ CHAPTER 17

22. Childhood guilt, adult depression? Jenny Chen, Jan 5 2015, The Atlantic, accessed 26 September 2017. https://www.theatlantic.com/health/archive/2015/01/childhood-guilt-adult-depression/384176/
23. Weighed down by guilt: Research shows it's more than a metaphor Michael Hotchkiss, October 8 2013, accessed 26 September 2017. https://www.princeton.edu/main/news/archive/S37/97/09G89/index.xml?section=topstories

Appendices

☐ MY EMOTIONAL ENTOURAGE: THE PEOPLE WHO PUT ME TOGETHER

○ **Elli Richter www.ellirichter.com**

Holistic life coach and co-creator of the Perfectionist Rehab program, Elli splits her time between America and Germany, as well as holding space for clients across the world though her virtual mentoring programs. A spark plug for change and 'compassionate bullshit cutter,' her website contains tools to help you to silence your inner critic and stop 'shoulding over' yourself.

○ **Yvonne Ferrell www.karmahealing.com**

A healer, empowerment counsellor and spiritual life coach, Yvonne specialises in addressing the imbalance in the mind and body, especially related to old trauma or stored emotions, which can manifest in your physical body. Offering face-to-face sessions in the UK or Skype distance healing for clients globally, she works closely with cancer patients, addiction, past life issues and all of life's challenges, which can show up in your body as dis-ease.

○ **Marie-Pierre Cleret www.mariepierrecleret.com**
A psychotherapist with a private practice in Sydney, Australia, Marie offers private consultations, and conducts therapeutic training workshops for organisations. As well as couples counselling and conflict resolution, she specialises in healing childhood wounds and has extensive experience in dealing with narcissistic traits, in either yourself or a family member. She aims to help people understand that they are not defined by their past, nor does it limit them.

○ **Sonja Bollnow www.goldendoor.com.au**
A hypnotherapist and empowerment facilitator who runs a private practice out of the Golden Door health retreat in the Hunter Valley, Sonja practises reiki, somatic healing, past life regression, inner child workshops and alchemical hypno-therapy to help people come home to themselves, especially after trauma or tragedy. She also offers intimacy training and voice dialogue programs, to help people communicate more authentically with the people who matter to them.

○ **Jacqueline Wharton**
www.separationanddivorceadvisors.com.au
A former city lawyer who also worked as a conflict expert for a top ASX company, Jacqueline is a holistic divorce coach who realises that separation is more than just paperwork. The founder of Separation and Divorce Advisors, she was inspired to launch the company after having to negotiate her own divorce, when she realised that couples need full

circle support, practically and emotionally. She tailors her guidance to suit every client, depending on their circumstances and needs.

☐ BOOKS TO HELP YOU HEAL

◌ **Dare to Live Miriam Subirana**

You can enjoy your happiness right now—don't waste a second. This is the message of Miriam Subirana's self-development guide to living without fear, living with wholeness and increasing the quality of your life. One in a series, she is also the author of Live in Freedom and Creativity to Reinvent Your Life, which focus on artistic self-expression as a way to release old trauma.

◌ **In the Light of Meditation Mike George**

The book I always recommend when anyone I know is interested in dipping their toes into meditation. Mike George, a spiritual teacher from the Brahma Kumaris Spiritual Centre, breaks down the basics of meditation and its benefits. This is the perfect starting point for learning the art of mindfulness and is a must-read for experienced meditators too. It comes with a CD of guided meditations.

◌ **Option B Sheryl Sandberg and Adam Grant**

More than a book, Option B is an organisation and online support group to help people face adversity, build resilience and find joy, even when life challenges them. Co-written by Sheryl Sandberg, COO of Facebook, whose husband died suddenly in 2015 leaving behind their two children. Sheryl has written honestly on social media about the shock of finding herself widowed. The book combines her personal insights with research from psychologist Adam Grant, an expert in resilience.

○ Daring & Disruptive Lisa Messenger

A sought-after speaker in the start-up scene, Lisa Messenger, founder of The Collective Hub, talks openly about the ups and downs of chasing your dreams and stepping outside your comfort zone. In Lisa's words, 'there are few areas of my life I haven't fucked up' and yet today she has overcome her demons and runs a global media empire. One book in a series about entrepreneurship, this will help you to find your 'why' and then your 'how.'

○ Well & Good Nat Kringoudis

A doctor of Chinese medicine, acupuncturist and holistic fertility specialist, Nat Kringoudis is the founder of women's health clinic, The Pagoda Tree. Her passion is helping women to reconnect with their feminine bodies and make their hormones happier. That doesn't mean it's all about babies! With nutritional advice, recipes and recommendations based on ancient Chinese medicine, this book will help you to live a fertile life—in mind, body and spirit.

○ The Universe Has Your Back Gabrielle Bernstein

I could recommend any of Gabrielle Bernstein's books, but this is the one I read most recently and which resonated most deeply. The 'Spirit Junkie' fills the book with personal anecdotes and universal lessons that she has uncovered on her path to freedom, joy and happiness. Opening with a panic attack she suffered during a yoga class, Gabrielle was forced to realise she needed to reconnect with her faith and compassion. She urges readers to stop chasing life—and truly live.

○ **Dream Birth Catherine Shainberg PhD**
Whether you're trying for a baby, pregnant, attempting to heal from a traumatic birth or simply interested in the healing power of dreams and mental imagery, this book offers practical exercises and guidance to activate the creative power of your mind and connect with the wisdom of your body. Starting with pre-conception, it helps people to decipher their 'dreamfield' and use it to identify their aspirations and desires. There are also meditative exercises for clearing womb traumas, especially after the loss of a child.

□ SUPPORT GROUPS (WITH A TWIST)

○ **One Wave Is All It Takes**
www.onewaveisallittakes.com
Every Friday at 6.30am on beaches across Australia, a gang of surfers run into the waves wearing ridiculous fluorescent outfits, from banana costumes to pink tutus (on the men!). Started by Bondi Beach locals, Grant Trebilco and Sammy Schumacher, One Wave Is All It Takes aims to raise awareness of mental health issues with their weekly event #FluroFriday. If strangers ask what they're up to, they use it as an opportunity to raise the issue of mental health and ask—are you okay? Swimmers, yoga lovers and spectators are all welcome. They also work with hospitals to include 'salt water therapy' in their treatment plans.

⌒ **Intrepid Landcare www.intrepidlandcare.org**
It can be hard to add ecotherapy into your life when you don't have anyone to adventure with. The Australian not-for-profit Intrepid Landcare, which has groups across the country, aims to bring together young people who want to get back in touch with nature, by running regular events where attendees help with environmental projects. This could involve pulling weeds from a glow-worm tunnel or kayaking to a hard-to-reach spot to do bush regeneration. No previous experience is necessary to take part. It's been shown that volunteering can reduce stress levels and boost happy hormones.

⌒ **Beard Season www.beardseason.com**
More of an awareness group than a support group, Beard Season's aim is to reduce the devastating effect of skin cancer, by encouraging people to have regular skin checks, to share their experience on social media and encourage others to do the same. This not-for-profit was created by advertising executive Scott Maggs, the beard behind Beard Season, who was inspired to launch the project after a friend died of malignant melanoma at the age of 26. The organisation's social media feeds are full of photos of people who found cancer early, because of the initiative.

⌒ **Brahma Kumaris www.brahmakumaris.org.au**
With retreat centres in over 110 countries and territories around the world, the Brahma Kumaris Spiritual Centre offers one-day courses, weekend workshops and online talks teaching meditation, mindfulness and spiritual development—and it's all free. This donation-supported

organisation teaches Raja meditation—an open-eyed meditation which makes is easy to practise anytime, anywhere. They also run programs teaching mindful eating and how to cope with the constant chatter of the modern world.

Acknowledgements

This book has been many years, many conversations and many lessons in the making, and there are so many people I have to thank for its creation. The team at Hay House Australia—Leon, Errin and Rosie—who answered my manifestation on Twitter, believed in my vision and turned an idea into reality.

Thank you to the incredible women who turned me from a young girl with a love of words into a writer. To Vicky for taking a chance on me, what feels like a lifetime ago; and Louisa for spending days, weeks and months teaching me how to craft. To Lisa and Mel at The Collective, for always giving me the freedom to work in a way that serves me; and to all the editors, deputy editors and publishers who have pushed me and given me opportunities I couldn't even dream about.

I also have to thank my emotional entourage: Yvonne my spiritual teacher, Elli my soul sister and Marie-Pierre, who took me on a therapeutic path I didn't even know I needed.

To my sister Louise, who I mention very little in the book because she is on an amazing journey of her own. You were the one who never gave up on me. Even though we live further away than ever, I've never felt closer to you. I love you.

To my dad, who taught me the meaning of resilience. To my mama, who bravely shares her story to break down the stigma of mental health issues. You both make me proud every day.

To the Laboyries, who made me part of the clan long before I took your name. You filled a space in my heart.

To the women who taught that you can be strong and soft, capable and compassionate, ambitious and loving— Marisa, Misha, Ally, Avis and the women I've watched from afar embracing their feminine power.

A special thankyou to the tribe at Milk & Honey cafe in Kiama, who gave me a creative home, a safe space and a sense of belonging. Thank you for your kindness, endless chai teas and for loving my baby girl like family.

To my special chosen one, who didn't heal me but completed me, who has taught me more about kindness, loyalty and empathy than any human I've ever known. You are incredible. Thank you for bringing me home.

To our baby girl who slept on my chest through the edits. I will never forget our writing dates and the creative peace and clarity you gifted me.

Finally, this book wouldn't have been possible without the hundreds of men and women who shared their experiences so generously with me over the years; the strangers

I've laughed with, cried with and spent hours on the phone with. The people who trusted me, even as a twenty-year-old, to put their stories into words. I hope this is only the beginning for us all.

About the Author

Amy Molloy, formerly editor of Grazia Australia, is a freelance journalist, author and editor who writes for the biggest names in Australian and UK publishing. At the age of 23, she signed her first book deal for her memoir Wife, Interrupted, which documented her experience of being widowed. As a ghostwriter, she has authored seven books, both fiction and non-fiction.

Currently a Contributing Editor at Collective Hub, she contributes to global publications including The Times, The Telegraph, The Guardian, Marie Claire, Harper's BAZAAR, Sunday Style and Women's Health Magazine.

Amy is a proud ambassador for 1 Million Women, a global movement of women and young girls speaking out on environmental issues. She splits her time between London and Sydney, where she lives with her husband and baby daughter.

Twitter: @amy_molloy
Instagram: @amy_molloy
www.amymolloy.com

We hope you enjoyed this Hay House book. If you'd like to receive our online catalogue featuring additional information on Hay House books and products, or if you'd like to find out more about the Hay Foundation, please contact:

Hay House Australia Pty. Ltd.,
18/36 Ralph St., Alexandria NSW 2015
Phone: +61 2 9669 4299 • *Fax:* +61 2 9669 4144
www.hayhouse.com.au

Published and distributed in the USA by: Hay House, Inc.,
P.O. Box 5100, Carlsbad, CA 92018-5100
Phone: (760) 431-7695 • *Fax:* (760) 431-6948
www.hayhouse.com® • www.hayfoundation.org

Published and distributed in the United Kingdom by:
Hay House UK, Ltd., Astley House, 33 Notting Hill Gate,
London, W11 3JQ • *Phone:* 44-203-675-2450
Fax: 44-203-675-2451 • www.hayhouse.co.uk

Published in India by: Hay House Publishers India, Muskaan Complex,
Plot No. 3, B-2, Vasant Kunj, New Delhi 110 070
Phone: 91-11-4176-1620 • *Fax:* 91-11-4176-1630
www.hayhouse.co.in

Distributed in Canada by:
Raincoast, 2440 Viking Way, Richmond, B.C. V6V 1N2
Phone: 1-800-663-5714 • *Fax:* 1-800-565-3770 • www.raincoast.com

Access New Knowledge.
Anytime. Anywhere.

Learn and evolve at your own pace with the world's leading experts.

www.hayhouseU.com

Free e-newsletters
from Hay House, the Ultimate
Resource for Inspiration

Be the first to know about Hay House's free downloads, special offers, giveaways, contests, and more!

 Get exclusive excerpts from our latest releases and videos from *Hay House Present Moments.*

 Our *Digital Products Newsletter* is the perfect way to stay up-to-date on our latest discounted eBooks, featured mobile apps, and Live Online and On Demand events.

 Learn with real benefits! *HayHouseU.com* is your source for the most innovative online courses from the world's leading personal growth experts. Be the first to know about new online courses and to receive exclusive discounts.

 Enjoy uplifting personal stories, how-to articles, and healing advice, along with videos and empowering quotes, within *Heal Your Life.*

 Have an inspirational story to tell and a passion for writing? Sharpen your writing skills with insider tips from *Your Writing Life.*

Sign Up Now!

Get inspired, educate yourself, get a complimentary gift, and share the wisdom!

Visit www.hayhouse.com.au to sign up today!

9 781401 950873